DON'T
PAY THE
RANSOM,
I've Escaped

Memories of a Life on the Radio

MIKE BENNETT

Hudson Valley Humor LLC

Hudson Valley Humor LLC

Book Designers: Amy Cole (text design) and Amy Landheer (cover design) of JPL Design Solutions, Wyoming, MI

Book Printer: Color House Graphics, Grand Rapids, MI

Book Specs: This perfect bound book is typeset using Bookman Old Style 12 point font with a 20 point leading for the body copy. The text stock is a 50lb antique natural text manufactured by Glatfelter and is SFI certified. The cover is printed full-color on 10ptC1S with a glossy lamination.

ISBN: 978-0-615-92217-1

Printed in the United States of America

TABLE OF CONTENTS

INTRODUCTION

INTRODUCTION, OF SORTS

My publisher recently called and asked me to write "an introduction, of sorts" for this book. When your publisher asks you to add a couple of hundred more words to a manuscript that's already 20,000 words long, you figure, okay, what the heck?

So now I will introduce the sorts. Because that's what he asked for: an introduction, of sorts. Over there are the little sorts, and over to the left are the big sorts. There are mixed sorts in those burlap sacks, and pink fluorescent sorts in the black plastic trash bags in the corner. I think that covers the "sorts."

As you thumb through this book, assuming of course that you have thumbs, you will note that most of my humor is self-referential. I often poke fun at myself, because I know that I won't fight back or start heckling myself. And if my self-directed humor gets really out of hand, I know that I'm too lazy to file a libel suit.

I like to say that I'm the butt of my best jokes, because I have a somewhat large butt and it's a great target. For humor, that is, not for anything else.

Moving right along, this is a humor book, and as such, it reflects my sense of humor, which happens to be fairly gentle. If you're looking for racy or raunchy humor, you'll have to wait for my next book.

Most of my humor revolves around or relates to the Hudson Valley region of New York state, which is where I grew up. It's also where I now work and live. I wish that I had a riveting backstory involving a troubled childhood on the steppes of Central Asia, running drug cartels in Central America and dancing with kangaroos in Australia, but no such luck.

Over the years, my humor has been described as wry, dry (as in dry rye toast, hold the seeds) and even, on occasion, bland. I hail from a school of comedy that seeks to soothe, rather than harm. That doesn't mean that I'm not capable of "killing an audience" (which is entertainment-speak for "getting laughs"), but I prefer to kill my audiences with kindness rather than napalm.

I'm okay with the occasional chuckle, an odd giggle or even a snort every now and then. Knee-slappers and side-splitters are not my specialty, and I seriously doubt that you will find yourself laughing so hard that you'll need to call a doctor. But if you have an oxygen tank handy, you can probably make it through the book without losing consciousness. Better still, get a tank of nitrous. Laughing gas is always your best friend, especially at funerals.

Another quick warning: This book is riddled with misinformation and exaggerations. In the spirit of making amends for multiple sins of ignorance, I have included a list of important historical events at the end of the book. Feel free to photocopy the list (or just tear it out of the book, but try not to destroy the binding) and bring it with you to your next history exam. Your teachers will love you, I promise ...

As you will discover in the semi-autobiographical sections of the book, I attended Monroe-Woodbury High School. MW, as we called it, was and still is, in Central Valley, which is a hamlet within the town of Woodbury, New York. But most of the kids who attended the school were from the neighboring town of Monroe, and I guess that's why it got top billing.

The old high school that I attended is now an elementary school. It sits on Route 32, across from Woodbury Common, the internationally famous (and that's no exaggeration!) outlet shopping destination. People from every corner of the world come to shop at Woodbury Common. Many of them arrive from Europe and the Middle East on charter "shopping flights" to JFK Airport, then take special buses from the airport to Woodbury Common. Frankly, I find it amazing. People also drive from all over the tri-state area to shop at Woodbury Common, which makes for some truly awful traffic jams.

Woodbury Common was built on a cow pasture across the highway from the high school. In the middle of the pasture was a big shade tree. Students would dash like crazy across the highway, head directly for the far side of the tree, and light up their cigarettes.

Every couple of minutes, a student would peer around the tree to see if the vice principal, Mr. Baumgarten, was watching. If the coast was clear, the students would dash back across the pasture, run across the highway and sneak back into school. The main goal (aside from not being spotted by Mr. Baumgarten) was to avoid stepping in a pile of cow poop while sprinting from the tree to the highway. It was also considered bad form to be hit by a truck while you were running across Route 32, but stepping in cow poop was generally considered the worst possible thing that could happen to a student.

Well, if the worst thing that happens to you while you're reading this book is that you step in some cow poop, consider yourself lucky. One of my relatives advised me to buy a liability policy – just in case someone leaves a copy of the book on the stairs, his mother-in-law trips over it on her way to the bathroom and the next thing you know I'm in court explaining why the book wasn't equipped with a blinking red light and a small siren.

Okay, that's the introduction, of sorts. I sincerely hope that you enjoy the rest of the book. And please, whatever you do, don't leave it lying around on the stairs or anywhere else where someone can trip over it and break their hip. Do we have an agreement? Are you with me on this?

Part One

LAKE TEGUCIGALPA

NO KINDERGARTEN TODAY

Thanks for reading this book. I appreciate your interest. Writing is quite an exercise. Talking is a lot easier. Especially when you have a microphone.

For me, talking for hours and hours and hours comes naturally. That doesn't mean that I have a lot to say. I don't really. When I'm on the radio, I talk mostly about the mundane details of everyday life. Such as traffic jams, bad weather and school closings.

When I meet people who grew up in the Hudson Valley, I usually don't have to introduce myself. I just say, "Newburgh, two-hour delay, no morning kindergarten." And then they usually say something like, "Oh, you're the guy on the radio ... Mike Bennett, right?"

My wife tells me that I mumble *"two-hour delay, no morning kindergarten"* in my sleep. That makes sense, I guess, although I'm usually asleep at the time so how would I know whether it makes sense or not? I could be mumbling the combination of the office safe or the recognition code words for the D-Day landing, I can't really say for sure.

At any rate, I've been saying things like that on the radio for the past 40-plus years. I can't imagine doing *anything* for 40-plus years, much less reading lists of school closings. Frankly, it just boggles my mind. But there it is. The story of my career in a nutshell.

I started doing radio in 1972. Looking back, it seems like 10,000 years ago. Or maybe more like 500 years ago. Did they have radio back then? Let me Google "Marconi," and I'll get right back to you. You all know who Marconi was? No, not the guy who invented pasta. He's the guy who invented radio. They called it wireless back then, because nobody wanted to trip over a bunch of wires.

That's the first thing you learn in the radio business: Don't trip over the wires. I can't tell you how many times a pizza delivery guy will come into the studio, trip over a wire and the station will go dead for three weeks while we all try to figure out which wire got yanked out of its socket.

Okay, that's completely untrue. First of all, we never get pizza delivered to the station. In fact, we never get any kind of food – be it Chinese, Indian,

Guatemalan, you name it – delivered to the station. We're here to work, not to eat. At least that's what the station manager tells us.

THE ALARM GOES OFF AT 4:45 A.M.

Talking on the radio is a great way to make a living. If you love it, you will enjoy it to the nth degree. They always say if you have a job that you love, it's not really work.

Well, it really *is* work. When you have to get up at 4:45 a.m. to go to work, that's work. But having said that, it's the best job I could have ever imagined.

I don't think I have any other skills, so there's not much else I could do. And I really do love what I do, each and every day.

People ask me all the time, "What time do you get up?" My alarm goes off at 4:45 a.m. But my alarm isn't what gets me out of bed – especially on cold winter mornings.

What gets me out of bed – even when I'm tired or there's a blizzard howling outside – is thinking about the show I'll be doing. When I wake up in the morning, the first conscious thoughts that pop into my mind are simple questions:

What are we going to talk about today?
Who are we going to interview?
What's going to be special about today's show?

Sometimes I also ask myself why I ate those extra helpings of sausage lasagna and wonder if eating all of that mocha-chocolate chip gelato right before going to sleep accounts for the weird dreams I've been having recently. But then my thoughts return to the day ahead.

After spending a couple of moments rehearsing the show in my mind, I know exactly why I want to get up and actually go to work. That doesn't mean that I dash to the front door and race over to the studio, but visualizing and imagining the show is what gets me out of bed and stumbling toward the bathroom. Even when you're on radio, you still have to take a shower and brush your teeth, at least occasionally.

COVERING THE NEWS

The great thing about radio is that every day is different. I covered the news for part of my career, and the news changes minute by minute. You can be sitting there daydreaming, and two seconds later, suddenly something dramatic happens. Unfortunately, it's usually something bad, but that's part of the job. Bad news travels fast, and your job is making sure that everyone gets the bad news as quickly as possible. Hmm, maybe covering the news wasn't such a great job after all.

But hey, it was a living. And honestly, I loved being the first person to know something that most other people didn't know. And I loved having the responsibility for conveying the news, accurately and objectively, to our audience. It was a great feeling. At least most of the time. When I covered really bad news, such as road accidents or house fires in which people died, then it wasn't so much fun. But if you don't mind an occasional disaster here and there, it's a wonderful job. I covered the news for 28 years, and I don't regret a minute of it.

One of my favorite news stories was the return of the U.S. Embassy hostages from Iran. They flew from Iran to Germany, and then from Germany to Stewart Air Force Base (now Stewart Airport) in Newburgh. No, Ben Affleck was not there, but it seemed like every news reporter in the world was in Orange County for what proved to be a heartwarming and highly emotional story.

From the airport, the ex-hostages were taken by bus to the U.S. Military Academy at West Point, which is probably one of the most picturesque spots in the Hudson Valley. As they traveled from Newburgh to Highland Falls (that's the town where West Point is located), the ex-hostages were greeted by huge crowds of well-wishers. It seemed as though every tree in Orange County had a yellow ribbon tied around it.

As an American and as a radio newsman, I was delighted. It was tough on my feet, however, since we had been forced to park our cars outside the academy grounds and West Point is a big place. I spent the next two or three days trying to get interviews with the ex-hostages, which required sprinting (with all of my radio gear) toward them whenever one or two of them appeared, and screaming, "Hi, I'm Mike Bennett and I'd like to interview you for WHUD!"

Compared with what they'd been through in Tehran, I'm sure that I didn't seem particularly threatening, but I don't recall that any of them seemed especially pleased to have microphones and cameras shoved in their faces by roving packs of journalists.

Blisters aside, it was a great experience – for them and for me. They were treated to unlimited quantities of ice cream and apple pie, and I covered the story of a lifetime. Not a bad deal.

MOVING TO THE MORNING SHOW

I dearly loved being a news reporter, but when the opportunity came to move from news into something more entertaining, I jumped at the chance. I will always remember my first day as co-host of The Morning Show on WHUD. It was March 20, 2000 – our son Michael's 13th birthday, coincidentally.

It's been a magical ride ever since. We're the No. 1 rated morning show in the nine counties considered part of the Hudson Valley radio market. Eight of those counties are in New York State, but one is in Pennsylvania. I don't know how it got in there – probably some backdoor deal dating back to the days of William Penn. I can't eat oatmeal without thinking of him. That's probably why I don't eat a lot of oatmeal. Don't get me wrong, oatmeal is good for you. Very healthy, I'm told. But if you're in the radio business, oatmeal – or any food that's incredibly high in fiber – is not a good idea. Email me if you don't know what I'm talking about.

But I digress. We were talking about radio markets. New York City is the No. 1 market and Los Angeles is the No. 2 market. The Hudson Valley is No. 39. Not bad. Over the past four decades, we've gone from being nothing to being the 39th-largest market in the United States. We're bigger than Albuquerque!

ROLLING ON THE RIVER

The Hudson Valley is a great place to live and work. We can hop on a train or get in a car, ride to New York City, walk downtown, take off our clothes and swim naked to the Statue of Liberty. Not that anyone would do that, but it's nice to think that you could indulge yourself if you really had the urge. It's a free country, and nobody in New York really cares what you do as long as you remember to tip the bartender.

The really nice thing about where I work is that there are always plenty of celebrities to interview – some of them actually live around here, and many others pass through while they're doing publicity tours. So there's never any shortage of interesting people around, and a good portion of them wind up on our show.

At the risk of repeating myself, which is something I do quite often, the station is perfectly situated. We're within driving distance of a major metropolitan area, which means that we can attract a steady flow of talented artists who don't mind answering nonsensical questions at ridiculously early hours of the morning. And thanks to the largely rural nature of the Hudson Valley, we also have an unlimited supply of ticks, bats and barn owls.

GAZING INTO MY CRYSTAL BALL ...

People frequently ask me to predict the future of radio, and to comment on the rise of satellite radio. So far, I haven't seen any evidence that satellite radio has affected us at all. I'm not saying that people don't listen to it, because obviously they do, but as far as my day-to-day job goes, nothing has changed since the introduction of satellite radio.

Personally, I have nothing against satellite radio. We don't compete against satellite radio. From my perspective, it's an entirely different kind of animal. For starters, satellite radio doesn't provide news about school closings, or local up-to-the-minute traffic and weather information. Traffic and weather are important to most people, and that kind of information needs to be delivered regularly on a local basis, which is something that satellite radio can't do very well.

Satellite radio also can't offer listeners free tickets to local events, which is something that I do practically every day. If there's a live music concert in Poughkeepsie this Friday, you know that I'll be offering free tickets to listeners who call in. At most, they might have to answer one or two simple questions to win the tickets. I usually avoid asking questions that would require an in-depth knowledge of quantum physics or details of the Kellogg-Briand Pact.[1]

---

1   A 1928 treaty signed in Paris that outlawed war. Thank goodness it worked.

What's seems strange to me is the number of radio stations that are fully automated. That's a scary trend. There's nobody at those stations. They use something called "voice tracking" that enables them to create four or five hours of programming in about 20 minutes. A disc jockey, who could be sitting in a studio thousands of miles away, reads off a script and the vocal patter is automatically inserted into the program by a computer.

Automation makes sense from a purely business perspective, but it doesn't make for good radio programming. That's my opinion – as of today. Radio is a business, and business is always changing. That's just the way it goes. You can roll with the punches, or you can get rolled over. Or you can eat a breakfast roll, and avoid the whole issue.

But seriously, the problem with the fully automated stations is that when something happens in your town, there's nobody to call. Imagine if a goat or a donkey wandered into your yard late at night. Who would you call? Not the radio station. Unless you live somewhere in the Hudson Valley, of course.

At WHUD and at our sister station K104, we have a person in the studio 24/7, all year round. Almost without exception, there is somebody there to pick up the phone. That's the value of local radio. If the bus bringing the cheerleaders back from a game breaks down on the Taconic Parkway, we'll tell you about it. Most listeners won't really care. But if you're a parent of one of those cheerleaders and you're waiting in the high school parking lot for the bus to arrive, then it's important news.

We call it "live and local," and it's a simple philosophy. We're committed to serving our local listeners. And as a result, they're committed to us. Of course some of them are also committed to institutions, but that's a different kettle of fish.

Sadly, our model is no longer the industry standard. But it works for us, and it works for our audience. Personally, I think it's a great model, and it's perfectly suited to my style of radio.

AN AUDIENCE OF ONE

When I'm talking on the radio, I don't imagine that I'm talking to a large audience – even though on some days, there can be more than a million people listening. I imagine instead that I'm talking to one person who is sitting right here in the studio with me. I can't see that person, and that person can't reply directly to what I'm saying, but in my mind, that person is sitting right there in front of me, listening carefully to every word that I'm saying.

Which basically means that I can't curse or swear. Not only would it violate our station's policy, it would be out of character for me. I don't normally curse or swear when I'm talking to people. Unless I've been drinking heavily, which, as a general rule, I try to avoid doing. Especially since my heart attack.

My heart attack was a wake-up call, for sure. I would like to say that it totally changed my life and that I became a teetotaling vegan, but that would be an outright fib. The biggest impact it had was on my vocabulary. Now I can use the words "myocardial infarction" in a sentence without stumbling. If you're ever trying to impersonate a cardiac surgeon, that's important.

I had my heart attack a couple of years ago. That's as close to death as I want to get for the time being. After you've had a heart attack, you appreciate everything about life much more. It really crystallizes your vision. It helps you see what's important and what's not. I'm certainly not suggesting that you go out and have a near-death experience. Especially if you have plans for the weekend.

MAJORING IN LUNCH

I graduated from Monroe-Woodbury High School in 1970. I know, that's a long time ago. Not as long ago as the Peloponnesian War, but almost. There were about 230 kids in our graduation class, and roughly half of them went to OCCC (Orange County Community College). Basically, none of us knew what we wanted to do with our lives. I was the biggest goof-off of them all; I had no clue whatsoever about anything. Did you like that semicolon?

Like many of my male college friends, however, I was aware that there was a war going on at the time, and I knew that if I didn't enroll in college, I would be subject to the draft. Being drafted into the military and going to Vietnam wasn't high on my list of priorities, so it made sense for me to enroll at OCCC, even though my only real reason for being

24

there was to prevent our local draft board from certifying me "1-A" and shipping me to Southeast Asia.

We don't have a draft today, so it's hard to imagine how much it weighed on our youthful minds. It wasn't that we were unpatriotic – heck, we all celebrated the Fourth of July by drinking beer and waving sparklers until we fell over – it was just that we didn't like the idea of people with authority – especially older people with authority – telling us what to do with our lives. We felt reasonably certain that given the means and the opportunity, we could mess up our lives all by ourselves, thank you very much.

At any rate, here I was at OCCC, with no idea why I was there. I would start my day in the cafeteria, find a bunch of my friends from high school, sit down with them and drink coffee until it was time for them to go to class. Then I would wait for another bunch of friends to arrive, and I would have coffee with them. I would do that pretty much all morning, until it was time for lunch. Fortunately for me, I was already in the cafeteria, so I was rarely late.

After lunch, I would stick around and chat with any of my high school friends who stopped by, then have a snack, drink more coffee and chat with more friends until it was time to go home. It was a rough schedule, but hey, no one ever said that college was easy.

To be fair, it was mostly pure fun. There were so many kids from Monroe-Woodbury at OCCC that I always had someone to talk with. And that's mostly all that I did when I was in college – sat in the cafeteria and talked with my friends.

Many of my friends actually graduated from OCCC and went on to four-year colleges. I was not one of them. As it turned out, the remarkably short-sighted administration at OCCC would not recognize the importance of my "lab work" in the cafeteria, and after a brief but amicable discussion at the end of the semester, we mutually agreed that it would be better for all parties if I did not return as a student.

They also asked me to settle up my outstanding parking fines, which I thought was asking too much. I was fresh out of Confederate money, or I would have paid them on the spot. They took my IOU instead, and with handshakes all around, accepted my resignation from the ivy-covered halls of academe. And that was the end of my college career. Boola boola, boola boola.

THE LEGEND OF 'BOARDS BENNETT'

I did manage to earn some legitimate academic credits at OCCC. Oddly, the credits were for taking a gym class. Which is really strange, because I never considered myself much of an athlete. As a little boy, I ran around barefoot a lot, but in the days before video games, running around barefoot was pretty much all there was to do.

When I got to high school, I played briefly on the freshman football team, but my unfortunate habit of throwing up after every wind sprint quickly put me in the dog house with the coach, who had problems of his own and didn't need me adding to them.

The pinnacle of my athletic adventuring took place during my junior year in high school, when I played defense on an ice hockey team, the oddly named New York Golds. The Golds played in a semi-nefarious organization that called itself the Monroe Hockey League. The MHL was sort of the French

Foreign Legion of sports. It accepted everyone who wanted to play, no questions asked.

Those were the days of wooden sticks, leather gloves and minimal protective padding. Helmets were considered a sign of cowardice, and for the life of me I can't remember anyone ever using a mouth guard. Everyone in the league had two or three missing teeth, various scars and strange twitches. We shared a sort of casual disregard for basic rules of sportsmanship, which made for some interesting games.

One of the things I really loved about the MHL was that the paperwork was practically nonexistent. Nobody checked your birth certificate or asked you for a valid form of government ID. As a result, most of the teams had a couple of tough old Canadians who claimed to have skated with Rocket Richard or Gump Worsley back in the era when hockey was "a real man's game" or words to that effect.

It was hard to tell exactly *what* they were saying because those geezers had *no teeth*, spoke with impenetrable French-Canadian accents and seemed to have an endless supply of cheap booze that they guzzled freely from heavily dented metal flasks hidden deeply within the folds of their sweat-encrusted hockey pants.

Despite their grumpy inscrutability, the old codgers were great to have around, especially since they were the only players who really seemed to understand the game, and they could skate rings around the rest of us.

Skating, sadly, was not my strong suit. I'm not going to blame my skates, which had been personally autographed by Hans Brinker sometime in the previous century, but they didn't help. My ankles were the real problem, though. It was as though I had been born without the ability to absorb calcium below my knees. My ankles had the consistency of whale blubber, and no matter how much tape I put on them, they always gave out after about 15 seconds of skating. That's why they called me "Boards Bennett," because I always tried to stay near the boards so I could grab onto them when I began collapsing.

In one particularly brutal game, there was a bench-clearing brawl in the third period. We were down by 26 goals, and our player-coach Basil (who was studying to become a Capuchin monk), instructed us to pick a player on the opposing team and "just go out there on the ice and kill him!" I don't know if that's the way they coach in the NHL, but in the MHL, it was par for the course. Or par for the rink, I should say. So, over the boards we went, ostensibly to seek and destroy our clearly more talented opponents.

I did a pretty good job of leaping over the boards, but after that, things went awry fairly rapidly. My ankles crumpled as soon as my blades hit the ice, and I went down like a sack of Portland cement. I don't remember whether I hit my head on the ice or not – does anyone really remember those kinds of details? – but I *do* remember having difficulty getting up.

Lying motionless on the ice, I was quickly surrounded by wizening oldsters muttering grimly in what I assumed was French, or maybe they were doctors speaking in Latin to spare my feelings. Everything was getting kind of hazy and if I didn't actually black out, I came pretty darn close.

Today, someone would have whipped out a cell phone, tapped 9-1-1 onto the keypad and within minutes an ambulance would have whisked me to a modern hospital with pretty nurses and lots of fancy diagnostic equipment for peering into my cerebellum and inspecting it for damage.

Back in those days, however, there were only two hospitals in the area with emergency rooms, and the general rule was not to wake up the nurses unless someone was truly on the edge of imminent death or related to a high-ranking member of the hospital staff. And if you'd mentioned the word "cerebellum," they would have had you arrested for impersonating a neurosurgeon.

At any rate, I was able to regain the use of my legs after a couple of weeks. One of the first things I did was toss my skates in the garage, where they would have remained to this very day if only we hadn't moved and sold the contents of the garage at a yard sale. So much for playing ice hockey.

TELLING STORIES

As you can tell by now, I love telling stories. For me, telling stories has always been more than just a hobby or a talent. On a human level, telling stories is what keeps us together – as friends, as families, as a species. Seriously, it's our ability to communicate that sets us apart from all the other animals. That and the funny hats we wear at birthday parties.

Stories are a medium for sharing information efficiently. The information that we hear in stories tends to stick around in our minds a lot longer than information we read in a textbook or hear in a classroom.

Some scientists think that our ability to speak and communicate with each other led to our triumph over the Neanderthals, another species of early humans. We were the Cro-Magnon, and essentially, we had the gift of gab. Those other guys, the Neanderthals, didn't talk much. They were bigger and stronger than us, but they didn't have our vocal abilities. So if one of us ran into a Neanderthal in a forest 60,000 years ago, we might've said, "Hey, your shoe is untied," or "Wow, that's some pterodactyl!" and then poked him in the eye with a stick while he was trying to figure out a snappy comeback.

And that, my children, is how we survived and invented fast food restaurants and reality television, while the Neanderthals vanished back into the caves and were never heard from again. The way I figure it is that talking on the radio is just an extension of our ancestors' abilities to talk to each other while running away from larger rival species. If you can talk, you can make plans. If you can make plans, you're already halfway to doing something great.

FROM CAFETERIA TO WINERY

In my early twenties (or late teens, I forget exactly which), my ability to make plans was more on the level of the Neanderthals than the Cro-Magnon. As mentioned previously, my college career was brief. In and out. Here's your hat, what's your hurry?

All I had to show for my brief time in college was a couple of parking tickets and a great night at the Red Garter Inn, which was right around the corner from the campus. The Red Garter was a wild place, but I'll save those stories for the triple-x-rated video. Just kidding. The video will be rated I, which stands for, "I honestly can't recall who owns those panties, your honor."

Since I didn't know what else to do after leaving college, I took a job working at a local winery. It was easily one of the best jobs I could imagine. If you're ever offered a job at a winery, by all means, take it. You won't regret your decision. Your liver might regret it, but you will cherish the experience. Or at least as much of it as you can remember.

Let me tell you a little story about working at the winery, which was in a lovely little town not far from where I grew up. We gave tours to people who visited the winery. At the end of each tour, the adults in the group were offered the chance to taste the various types of wine we made. The tastings took place in our aptly named tasting rooms.

On average, the tour groups had about 20 people. Some groups had more, some groups had less. According to federal law, we had to keep an accurate tally of the number of people in each tour group.

Somehow, the management team at the winery saw fit to entrust me with the responsibility of keeping the daily tally. But the job wasn't as simple as it initially looked. The law also said that we had to reconcile the number of people who took tours with the number of empty wine bottles in the tasting rooms that people visited at the end of the tours. It had something to do with taxes. Up to a point, you could serve the wine without paying the tax. But after a certain point, you had to pay the tax.

Are you following all of this? I hope you are, because I'm already confused, and I worked there.

So at the end of the day, I'd sit there with an adding machine, a ledger book and dozens of wine bottles. All I needed was a green visor. By law, each adult who took the tour was allowed to "taste" eight ounces of wine. If they drank more than eight ounces, the winery would have to pay federal taxes on the additional amount they drank.

At the beginning of the day, we counted the bottles – some of them had been partially consumed the day before – and calculated the ounces of wine remaining in each bottle. At the end of the day, I examined each bottle, tried to figure out how many ounces were left in the bottle, and then totaled it all up. Then I took the number of people who had taken tours and compared it with the number of ounces that had been "tasted." To this day, it hurts my head just thinking about it!

Those numbers all had to match up, or Eliot Ness and the Untouchables would have swarmed the place and shut us down. That's what we believed, and nobody wanted to find out the hard way whether the federal government really cared or not. We figured that the law is the law, and we were going to follow it, no matter how silly it seemed. Yes, I realize that notion seems quaint today, but this was another time, long ago and far, far away ...

The problem was that on most nights, the numbers didn't even come close. There always seemed to be too much wine left over. So every Friday afternoon, right after the last official tour of the day, there would be a special party for the employees. If there had been ten tours that day, we would become the eleventh tour. And we would drink the remaining wine until the numbers matched up the way they were supposed to.

Those parties were lots of fun. Everyone had a good time, and we felt as though we were doing our duty as responsible, law-abiding citizens. I also remember that someone always brought cheese and crackers. Because when you're drinking wine, you've got to have cheese and crackers. It's an immutable law of nature.

MY SHIP ARRIVES!

So there I was, working at the winery, doing odd jobs and waiting for something to happen. At one point, I was driving a forklift and accidentally pinned my boss against the wall with one of the forks. Luckily for both of us, I didn't kill him. But that incident taught me an important lesson: When you're driving a forklift, make sure that you know how to shift it into reverse.

One evening, after a hard day of driving the forklift, I picked up a matchbook from the floor. This was back in the days when everyone smoked, all the time, so it wasn't unusual to find matchbooks all over the place.

But this wasn't any old matchbook. This matchbook turned out to be the key to my future. On the front of the matchbook was a tiny advertisement for a school that taught people how to drive tractor-trailer rigs. I was about to toss it in the trashcan when for some reason – there must have been a good angel hovering nearby – I turned over the matchbook and glanced at the back cover. That simple action changed my life. On the back cover of the matchbook was an ad for Announcer Training Studios in Manhattan. It said, "Learn How to Be a Radio DJ."

Somewhere in my brain, a light flickered on. *This is for me*, I said to myself. *This is something I can do!*

Yes, that matchbook saved my life and sent me down the path to success. Who knows, maybe I would have made more money driving tractor-trailers. But after my experience with the forklift, I figured it was probably not a good idea for me to become a professional driver.

I hopped onto the next available bus to Manhattan and quickly found myself at the Announcer Training Studios on West 48th Street. The school's most famous graduate was Sue Simmons, who anchored one of the local television news programs for about seventy years. Some of you may remember her, but if you don't, that's okay. People come and go in this business, so it doesn't pay to get sentimental. Especially about people that you don't even remember.

HERE'S YOUR DIPLOMA; NOW SCRAM!

The Announcer Training Studios was a vocational school. They gave you three months of training, handed you a diploma and shooed you out the door. The school no longer exists – there's a papaya juice franchise there now, I think – but it was there for me at just the moment that I really needed something to get me going in the right direction. The school's operating principle was, "We don't care if you have any talent, just give us your money."

A sound policy if there ever was one. And thanks to their enlightened nonjudgmental philosophy, virtually no one who attended the school had any talent. Some of the people in my class could barely speak. One guy was clearly psychotic and whispered furtively in some kind of strange gibberish. He's probably the head of CBS by now.

The important thing was that we learned what we needed to know to pass the FCC test and get our licenses – yes, you need a license to talk on the radio. We learned all the critical technical aspects of radio: how to turn on the transmitter, how to increase the power, how to lower the power and how to turn off the transmitter. That was pretty much it.

As I'm typing this, I can see that "transmitter" is a silly word. I wonder about its derivation. I know that "trans" means across, and I assume that "mitt" either refers to a baseball glove or a former presidential candidate. At any rate, that's the extent of my technical knowledge. If you need to know more, call Marconi.

As I said, the course lasted three months. At the end of the course, we made audition tapes (those were the days of reel-to-reel magnetic tape recorders) and sent the reels of tape, along with our incredibly flimsy résumés, to radio stations all over the country. And then we waited to hear back from them ...

A HELPFUL DETOUR

My mom and my step-father had put up the cash for the training course. Despite (or perhaps because of) my excellent work at the winery, I had no money of my own. From everyone's perspective, it seemed like a good idea for me to spend some time working at my step-father's real estate office, paying off my debt to society, as it were.

I would sit in his office, daydreaming about my career in radio, and answer the phone when someone called. When my step-father saw that I was capable of answering a telephone and saying something reasonably intelligent to the caller, he had an idea. Here's what he said: "Michael, you should get your real estate license. That way, if anybody wants to see a house, you can show it to them legally. And if you ever actually sell a house, you would receive a commission."

The magic word was "commission," which I correctly associated with cash money. He didn't have to say it twice, I got the picture. I studied for the test and passed it with flying colors. Oddly, I never sold a house. But having a license to sell real estate got me my first job in radio. Makes sense, right?

Here's how it happened: My résumés landed on the desk of the manager of a small station in Hyde Park. When he saw that I held both an FCC license *and* a real estate license, he assumed that I must be some sort of multi-talented genius. More to the point, he figured that he would get a radio announcer and an advertising salesman rolled into one affordable package.

I went for an interview ... and was hired! Here was the deal: On the weekends, I would broadcast the news. During the week, I would sell ads. Or more accurately, I would *try* to sell ads. My sales territory was the city of Kingston. If you look at a map, you can see that Kingston is near Hyde Park. But the radio station's 500-watt signal was too weak to reach Kingston. Even if they'd wanted to, the people there couldn't listen to our programs. It's not like today, when you can listen to most any radio station on the Internet.

The fact that people in Kingston couldn't hear our programs – heck, I don't even think they knew we existed – would have made it difficult for even the most polished salesman to sell ads. My lack of sales experience made a bad situation even worse.

I remember walking into a lumber yard, all dressed up, with no appointment. It was a typical cold call, you just walk in and say hello to everyone until you find the manager. At least I looked the part. I was wearing a suit and a tie. I eventually found the manager, and said, "Hi, I'm Mike Bennett from WHVW in Hyde Park Radio."

He said, "Huh? *What* station?" It quickly became apparent to me that he had never heard of us. That was a bad sign. I shouldn't have been surprised. If he'd driven to Hyde Park and sat in our driveway, he probably would've had trouble picking up our signal.

Undeterred (another great word that looks silly right after you type it), I pressed on, asking, "You don't want to buy some radio advertising, do you?" His reply wasn't especially promising: "Nope," he said.

43

I told him that I'd be back in a couple of months in case he changed his mind. Almost all of my sales calls followed a similar script. I'm surprised that no one called the cops and accused me of impersonating a salesman.

ON THE AIR, AT LAST

My first week as an ad salesman was uneventful, unprofitable and unpromising. But I still had the weekend to look forward to. That's when I would do my first shift *on the air!*

I didn't know what to expect, and neither did the station. Luckily, because I started on a Saturday morning, there were even fewer people listening than usual. Here's where all the intensive training that I had received at Announcer Training Studios came to bear. I keyed the microphone and, in my carefully practiced baritone Top-40 radio announcer voice, said, *"Good morning, I'm Mike Bennett, 95 WHVW in Hyde Park. Three people are homeless after a fire last night that began in their garage and spread rapidly through the rest of the house. No injuries were reported, but the house was heavily damaged and may have to be demolished ..."*

The station manager was so impressed with my on-air skills that within five months I was promoted to news director – full-time, not just on weekends! I think it helped that I was a terrible ad salesman and that the previous news director had been a hopeless alcoholic. I found dozens of empty bottles stashed in his desk after he left. I wish I was making up that part of the story, but it was true.

My radio career began on that Saturday morning in Hyde Park, and I've been talking pretty much non-stop ever since. Just ask my wife and family. Or tune your radio to 100.7 AM and listen to *Mike & Kacey* in the Morning on WHUD. You'll hear me blabbering away about something, I'm sure of that. Shooting the breeze isn't just my job – it's my life.

And that, my friends, concludes Part One of this book. Observant readers will note that there has been no mention of Lake Tegucigalpa. That is as it should be. The less said about Lake Tegucigalpa, the better.

Part Two

WHY I LOVE MY JOB,

REALLY!

FUN AND MAGIC

I'm not going to lie to you. Being on the radio is about the most fun you can have with your clothes on. I mean, think about it: The hardest part of my job is saying words into a microphone. Short words. *While sitting in a cushy chair.* Anybody with a larynx and a halfway decent set of glutes can do it.

Of course, there's more to it than that: Several times a day, I have to push some buttons, causing music to play. From time to time, I'm faced with the grueling task of chatting with the beautiful people who make that music. Other crushing responsibilities include telling jokes (some of which are actually funny – although past performance is no guarantee of future results) and giving away free tickets to upcoming concerts. Oh, and every couple of weeks, I have to log onto my online account to make the sure that the station has deposited my paycheck. Remind me what FICA stands for?

But to be honest, if the money, the mic and the cushy chair were the only things motivating me to haul my butt out of bed in the dead of night six times a week, I'd have left the business long ago. The thing that keeps me showing up is this:

In addition to having fun, I have the privilege of doing nice things for people every day of my working life.

That probably sounds pretty hokey in this age of irony, cynicism and general snarkiness, but it's the God's honest truth. I like doing nice things for people. I'm not talking about giving away concert tickets here. I'm talking about changing people's lives. All from the comfort of that cushy chair I was telling you about.

Let me give you an example. Every year on May 6th, it's National Nurses Day. It's a wonderful thing. People call in to nominate their favorite nurse, whether it's an RN at the doctor's office, their school nurse, a visiting nurse, whatever. So one day, about five years ago, we remind listeners that it's National Nurses Day. The phone calls start flooding in, as usual. People love their nurses! We're rattling off all these names, and we can hardly keep up with the flow. At one point somebody calls and says she'd like to nominate Mary Margaret Montgomery. Not exactly a name you hear every day. (In truth, I can no longer remember her name precisely, but I recall that she had three names and they all began with an "m.")

About an hour later, after most of the Nurses Day hubbub has settled down, the phone rings. The guy on the other end of the line says, "I don't know exactly how to go about this, but I heard a name on the radio this morning and I'm trying to confirm that that's what I heard." Now, it's not like we're tabulating results or anything. We've basically got a bunch of notes scribbled on Dunkin' Donuts napkins, which we've filed meticulously in random places around the studio. But just in case, I ask him what name he thought he heard. He said, "Mary Margaret Montgomery." I didn't need to refer to any notes. I let him know that I had indeed uttered that name earlier that morning.

There was a silence. Then the guy said, almost in a whisper, "Oh my God." Then, after another pause: "That's got to be my nurse."

Turns out, this guy was very sick when he was six years old. This is about 25 years earlier. They brought him to the hospital, close to death, and this one nurse singlehandedly brought him through it. "I was just a little boy," he said, "and I was scared. And then, there was this most fantastic nurse. When I heard her name on the radio, it triggered so many great memories."

Now *I'm* getting a little misty. I say, "Okay, let me call the doctor's office where they said she worked." At this point, I'm going through the trash trying to find my notes. I locate the correct napkin and I make the call.

"Is this Mary Margaret Montgomery?"

She confirms that she is, indeed, Mary Margaret Montgomery. So, I tell her the story. Now *she's* getting emotional. She goes, "Oh my God, I remember him!"

I say, "Well, we've got a match. He wants to talk to you. Is it all right to give him your number?" Long story short, they meet up, their families meet, they have lunch, everybody has a great time and he gets to thank her personally and tell her how much she meant to him all those years ago.

In radio, there's this one word that gets bandied about a lot by marketing types. The word is "reach."

When used by marketers, it refers to a whole bunch of measurable quantities. It's very scientific. Please stifle your urge to yawn.

For me, it means a lot more than just some demographic mumbo jumbo. To me, reach is epitomized by that little boy, all grown up now, hearing a name on the radio and being transported back in time. It's him calling up and wanting to thank her. It's the boy, now grown up, and his family, and the nurse and her family, all sitting down for sandwiches and soda and gratitude.

That's reach. And that's why I love my job.

A couple of pages ago, I wrote that radio is the most fun you can have with your clothes on. Then it occurred to me: I *could* be naked, and you'd have no idea! I mean, don't worry. I'm not naked. It's pretty cold in the studio. But still. I *could* be naked. And you'd have no way of knowing.

A BRIAN CASHMAN STORY

This story begins in the late 1990s. I can't remember the exact year. I'm doing a charity event in Rockland County, a fundraiser for a local organization. One of the featured guests is Brian Cashman, the general manager of the New York Yankees. Recently there had been an article about Cashman in one of the regional newspapers, the Times Herald Record, and the article mentioned that Cashman had grown up in Washingtonville, which isn't far from Highland Mills, which is where I grew up. I interviewed Cashman at the event, and I asked him about growing up in Washingtonville. He spoke briefly about his pleasant memories of Washingtonville, and then we moved on to another topic. We aired the interview a couple of days later, and that was that.

Fast forward five or six years. I'm signing calendars at a charity event in Newburgh, and a guy walks up with a manila envelope. He says, "I really enjoyed that interview you did with Brian Cashman a few years ago, and I'm really glad that you guys talked about Washingtonville." Then he opens the envelope and takes out an old class picture, the kind where all the kids are sitting on benches and smiling. It turns out that he was Brian's third-grade teacher in Washingtonville. Hearing the interview had jogged his memory, and he had looked through piles of class pictures until he discovered the picture of Brian's class.

Then the teacher asks me for a favor. He says that one of the kids in Washingtonville had lost his dad in the September 11 attacks and has been depressed ever since. The kid is a Yankees superfan, and the teacher asks me if I can get some Yankee memorabilia from Cashman. Now the plain truth is that I spoke with Cashman for less than ten minutes. But the teacher assumes that we're friends, because he heard us talking together on the radio. So I say, "Sure, I'll call him up and we'll see what happens. But I can't make any promises."

When I get back to the station, I call the Yankees' PR office, introduce myself (because frankly, they don't know me from a hole in a wall) and tell them the story. A month goes by, and I get an email from the teacher. Cashman has sent the kid a big package containing all kinds of cool Yankee gear. There's a hat, a ball, a signed team picture, and a personal note from Cashman telling him how much the team appreciates the kid's support. In his email, the teacher describes how kid really brightened up when he opened the package and that getting a personal note from Cashman made him feel like the entire Yankees organization was reaching out to him.

I'm not exactly sure what the moral of this story is, but it's a nice story and it reveals how radio often works in mysterious ways. And it also shows that no matter what anybody thinks about him in his role as GM of the Yankees, Brian Cashman is a mensch!

CELEBRITIES

I have interviewed thousands of celebrities. Most of them are happy to chat with me on the air for a couple of minutes about their latest CD, book, movie, TV show, road tour, art exhibit, marriage, divorce, court date or pending dental work.

You name it – if a celebrity does it, I'll have them on the program to talk about it. It's good for them and it's good for me. One hand washes the other. Sometimes it's more like, "I'll scratch my back and you scratch your back." If that doesn't make sense to you, don't worry. It doesn't make sense to me either. But that's the radio business for you.

Interviewing celebrities can be fun, especially when it's someone I admire or someone who is genuinely funny. My very first "celebrity inter-view" was with blues legend BB King. Since then, I've had great conversations with, in no particular order: Josh Groban, Donald Trump, Jon Stewart, Lisa Kudrow, Simon Cowell, Regis Philbin, Mary Tyler Moore, Sir Michael Caine, Geena Davis, Jane Fonda, Eli Manning, Mark Messier, Gladys Knight, Alan Alda, Tom Selleck, Mary Higgins Clark, Phil Collins, Darryl Hall, Glenn Frey, Linda Ronstadt, Heidi Klum, Ed McMahon, John Ritter, George Carlin and Bill Cosby.

I've picked up some great stories from celebrity interviews, even when the celebrities aren't house-hold names or super-famous. For instance, when I interviewed director John Sayles, he told me that he had initially offered actor John Cusack the role of the shortstop Swede Risberg in "Eight Men Out," Sayles' movie about the 1919 World Series scandal.

But Cusack turned down the part because he didn't think that he could execute a credible double play. Later, when the actor who had been cast as third baseman "Error-a-Day" Weaver dropped out, Cusack agreed to join the production, figuring that it would be easier to play a third baseman than a shortstop.

For some reason, that story tickles my funny bone. I think that John Cusack is a terrific actor who can probably play any role imaginable. But he was worried that he wouldn't do a good job playing the team's shortstop. Me, I would have taken any part that John Sayles offered me, but that's the difference between me and Cusack. He's a real actor and I'm a ham.

When I interviewed comedian Rob Schneider, he mentioned that his father got him started in show business. He told me that when he was in junior high, he read about a local comedy club that had an open tryout every Monday night. All you had to do was show up with some material and they would let you go up on stage. He told his dad, and his dad encouraged him to give it a try. Rob's dad even drove him to the comedy club. The rest, as they say, is history.

Some celebrities reveal their true colors under difficult circumstances. Here's a story I love: The singer Patty Smyth ("Goodbye to You," "The Warrior") was scheduled to call me for a live interview on the show. She was performing at a local venue, and we had been promoting the interview all morning. The time comes for her to call – and she doesn't call. We're just sitting there and waiting for the phone to ring, which it doesn't.

Okay, those kinds of things happen every now and again, but you always remember it when somebody burns you like that.

After the show, she calls. She had overslept and she was embarrassed. But this is where it becomes a great story. She says, "I'll make it up to you. Where's your studio?" To make a long story even longer, Patty and her guitarist played live in our studio in Fishkill. It was a wonderful experience, and it was much more fun than if we had just spoken on the phone.

Her willingness to go the extra mile – or in this case, go many extra miles – was very cool and I will always remember her as a great performer.

How she stays married to John McEnroe – yes, they are married – is a total mystery. Well, not really. I did a charity art auction with him after a tennis tournament. In real life, he's exactly the same as the guy you see on TV. Impatient, brilliant and very effective. Sort of like George S. Patton, only without the polished steel helmet.

When I interviewed Susie Essman, who plays Larry David's agent's wife on HBO's "Curb Your Enthusiasm," she told me that Martha Stewart had asked her a favor. "She wanted me to fix her up with Larry. She really meant it," said Susie.

I asked her if Martha would be too intimidating for Larry. Susie told me that when she mentioned Martha's interest in a date to Larry, he just laughed. Apparently, the "real" Martha Stewart is a genuinely lovely person and, once you get to know her, not intimidating at all. "But in a million years I can't see her with Larry David," said Susie. I can't see them together either, but stranger things have happened.

I vividly remember interviewing comedian Robert Klein at an event to support Riverkeeper, an organization dedicated to protecting the Hudson River. It was raining, and Klein did his best to keep everyone's spirits up, mostly by joking about the lousy weather. He also took a playful poke at the station, saying, "You can't go into the dentist's office without hearing WHUD."

Klein lives in Westchester, and spoke passionately about the need to maintain the Hudson and its surrounding environment. He also offered to teach "I Can't Stop My Leg," his hilarious take on blues music, to The Bacon Brothers (a band featuring actor Kevin Bacon and his composer brother Michael), who were also appearing at the Riverkeeper event. Klein proceeded to demonstrate various tempos at which the song could be performed, which got me laughing so hard that I nearly choked.

Like all entertainers, Klein couldn't resist promoting his own material, calling the recent release of his numerous HBO comedy specials a rare chance for fans to watch him age from "youth to geezer in one handy DVD set." Klein seems to have aged nicely, and his unique blend of Borsht Belt slapstick and subtle intellectual humor still works amazingly well. He cracked me up, for sure.

AND WHILE WE'RE ON THE SUBJECT ...

Quite a bit has been written about our apparently non-stop fascination with celebrities and our so-called "celebrity culture." Some scientists believe that our fixation with celebrities is deeply wired into our brains. In other words, we can't help ourselves. It started off millions of years ago, when we were living in small groups. Dad would say to his kid, "Hey kid, pay attention to Grnumf, he can really throw a spear!" This wasn't just idle interest. Grnumf's talent for throwing a spear meant there was more antelope meat on his table than anyone else's.

Pretty soon, all the dads were telling their kids, "Watch Grnumf and maybe you'll learn something from him." Before you know it, Grnumf is a celebrity and he's getting complimentary tickets to the woolly mammoth races. Sure, the seats were large jagged rocks and not too comfortable, but times were tough back then. These were the days before anyone had thought of inventing corporate skyboxes.

At any rate, back then, if somebody was good at something, you paid attention. If you paid attention, you had more food, you lived longer, and you had more kids. That's how we all evolved into celebrity-watchers. It's in our genes. Good luck explaining that to the next person who asks you why you're watching a Miley Cyrus video.

THE HAZARDS OF BEING A 'LOCAL CELEBRITY'

Generally, it's nice when people recognize my voice or, more rarely, my appearance. Being a quasi-celebrity (or a demi-celebrity) is almost all good. I say almost because in my case, people usually recognize me when they see me doing something foolish or embarrassing. This was especially true when my kids were younger.

Here was a typical scenario: I'd be shopping at the grocery store, with the kids. The kids, being kids, would misbehave and I would yell at them. At that exact moment, another shopper would look up from her cart, look at me quizzically for a moment and then say to *her* kids, "Oh look, there's Mike Bennett, from the radio." Fortunately, she did not add, "And he's publicly threatening to murder his children with a soup can." I knew that she was probably thinking that, but was too polite – or too afraid – to say it out loud.

When I took the kids to McDonald's, I could usually count on someone interrupting our meal to talk about something they'd heard me say on the show that morning or the day before. And they would expect me to amplify on some comment that I had made earlier that day or earlier that week, while managing my kids and gobbling down a Big Mac.

Now if there are three things I cannot do at the exactly the same time, it's yell at my kids, chew a hamburger and expand meaningfully on something that I can't even remember saying when I was half-awake at 5:30 in the morning. But that never stopped total strangers from wandering over to my table to make idle conversation. Usually, they would start with something like, "Hi Mike, I'm sorry to interrupt your meal, but ..." and then they would proceed to interrupt my meal.

The other problem about celebrity, at least for me, is that I usually dress like a slob when I'm not actually working. I mean, I tend to look seriously awful. Homeless guys offer to help me. I look like a garbage truck wearing a t-shirt and sandals. Well, maybe not that bad. But you get the idea. And that's my problem with semi-celebrity – it provides a steady supply of excruciatingly embarrassing moments when someone recognizes me and then recoils in horror because I look like a larger, older version of Carl from "Caddyshack."

So when someone asks me what it's like to be a local celebrity, I tell them that like almost everything else in life, it's a mixed blessing. Most of the time it's very nice, and sometimes it's not so nice. But it's what I do for a living, and I feel very fortunate, so I really can't complain. But if you see me wolfing down a sandwich at the lunch counter of a local diner, please wait until I've swallowed before you start talking to me. I will appreciate your manners and I'll be less likely to spit food all over you while we're chatting.

THE ADVANTAGES OF RADIO

And that reminds me of another advantage of being on the radio: you rarely spit food (accidentally or on purpose) at the people you're speaking to. There are two reasons for that: One, we try not to bring food into the studio because it tends to make a mess and, let's be honest, the studio owners pay us to speak, not to eat. Two, the people we speak to aren't actually in the studio – they're spread out all over the Hudson Valley, and, thanks to the Internet, all over the world.

As I mentioned earlier, when I'm speaking into a microphone I tend to imagine that I'm speaking to one person, and not to hundreds of thousands of people, or on some days, millions of people. Here's an odd thing: Even though I know better, when I listen to the radio I think that the announcer is speaking just to me.

I guess that's part of the illusion and the magic of radio. It's not really a one-to-one experience, but it feels like someone is talking directly to you. Or if you're the one with the microphone, it feels as though you're talking to just one person. It's crazy, but it's also true. When you're having a good day, you can really connect with people.

THE OPPOSITE OF BEING A SECRET AGENT

I'm on the radio four and a half hours a day, six days a week. After 40 years in the business, I don't have many secrets. The more you talk, the more you reveal yourself. It's only natural, right? As you can imagine, I do a lot of talking, and there is very little about myself that I haven't revealed over the years.

The good thing, of course, is that I'm not working for the State Department or the CIA, so I don't know anything that's worth keeping secret. My favorite TV shows, my favorite sports teams, my favorite musicians, my favorite kinds of pizza ... none of that stuff is exactly classified material.

Sometimes I would say something on the radio that embarrassed my kids – because I would talk about them on the show, usually bragging about something impressive they had accomplished or a good deed one of them had done for a neighbor – and they would complain that I was ruining their lives by blabbing about them to the world. Okay, I happen to believe they are the best three kids in the world. I imagine that most parents feel that way about their kids. The only difference is that I get to share my feelings with anyone who owns a radio (or any kind of digital device with Internet access) and who happens to be listening.

WHERE DOES THE TIME GO?

What's really strange, though, is when listeners tell me how much they enjoyed a particular story about my kids that I told 15 or 20 years ago. In their minds, my kids are still in diapers or waiting for the school bus.

In reality, my children – I should say, "our children," since my wife's role in this enterprise was obviously essential – are fully grown up. In fact, our daughter just had *her* first child, which makes us feel extremely blessed and extremely old.

Watching my daughter go through her pregnancy was probably the strangest event of my life. I couldn't wrap my head around the fact that "our baby" was going to have her own baby. But she did, and now we are officially grandparents. Does that qualify us for an additional tax break?

But seriously, being a grandparent is wonderful. The baby is fabulous, and I don't have to change her diapers. (Full disclosure: My wife sometimes changes the baby's diapers while I find an excuse to slip outside.)

MEANINGFUL CONNECTIONS

Interviewing celebrities (and occasionally acting like a celebrity) can be fun and cool, but that's not what keeps me in radio. Here's a true (and very rambling) story that will show you, hopefully, why I stay in this crazy business.

The story begins in 1996. I was emceeing (or is it MC-ing?) the annual Westchester Medical Center Ball. It's a huge gala event. I guess you might call it lavish, if you use words like that in everyday conversation. Let's just say that it's very fancy.

I'm standing there with my microphone, of course. I have a list of people to introduce, and I introduce a couple named Fareri. Naturally, I pronounce it "Ferrari," but they don't seem to mind. The Fareris stand up and begin sharing the story of how their daughter, Maria, got very sick one day, and how nobody could figure out what was wrong.

They took her to the local hospital, but she kept getting sicker. When it became evident that she needed more help than was available at the local hospital, she was rushed by ambulance to the Westchester Medical Center.

I'm listening to them tell this story and I'm thinking that it's going to have a happy ending. But I'm wrong. It turns out that Maria had rabies – she was bitten by a bat – and by the time it's diagnosed, the poor girl is dying. Maria was about the same age as my daughter, and I'm seeing my daughter's face in my mind as I'm listening to the Fareris tell their story.

I'm standing up at the dais, holding my microphone and fighting back tears. Maria's condition worsens, and she dies. Now everybody in the audience is in tears, and rightfully. The ballroom is silent, except for the sounds of weeping.

The Fareris announce that they intend to raise $25 million to build a free-standing pediatric hospital at the medical center. The audience is now smiling and applauding. As the emcee, I move on to the next item on the program. But at my first break, I literally ran over to the Fareris – whom I did not know from Adam, believe me – and told them that I would do anything I could to help them raise the money. I don't have much cash, I said, but I have spare time and I'm happy to donate my time to your cause. If you have an event you'd like me to MC, I'll be there. I'll never say no.

I spent the next six years helping the Fareris raise money to build the Maria Fareri Children's Hospital at Westchester Medical Center. I did about 60 events with them, everything from wine tastings to bachelor auctions to bicycle races to parties with the New York Yankees. I even emceed the ground-breaking ceremony when they actually began build-ing the new hospital!

And I learned something really important about life. You really cannot measure your success by material wealth. I never made a dime from those events, but they were so emotionally rewarding that I would do every one of them all over again if I had the chance.

But the story doesn't end there. Years later, my niece got very sick. She was 19 at the time, and attending college at Seton Hall. Similar to the situa-tion with Maria Fareri, nobody could figure out what was wrong with her. Some doctors thought she had a stroke, others suspected a bacterial illness. She wasn't responding to treatment, and she wasn't get-ting better. It was very frightening.

My brother and his wife took her to Maria Fareri Children's Hospital. They were praying for a miracle. Then they saw something that made them smile, and gave them fresh hope: On a wall of their daughter's room, they saw a plaque inscribed with these words: "This room donated by Mike Bennett and the WHUD listeners." My brother called me and said, "I think it's a good omen – we're in the WHUD room!"

Fortunately, this story has a happy ending. It turned out that my niece had picked up a strange kind of virus. When it was properly diagnosed, they could give her the right treatment. It took her almost a year to recover, but she eventually returned to college and graduated. The hospital definitely played a critical part in her recovery, and it makes me feel great to know that I contributed in a small way to the hospital.

MY HEART ATTACK

Ah, yes. I remember it well. It was Oct. 23, 2010, about a month after our daughter's wedding. I was in my car, heading for the station's annual Halloween costume ball in Tarrytown. I was passing through Cold Spring, which is a lovely town, very picturesque, with panoramic views of the Hudson River. I was feeling absolutely fine, right up until the moment when I felt like an 800-pound Sumo wrestler had suddenly placed a very heavy oblong box on my chest and was pushing down on it with all his strength, trying his best to stop me from breathing. It was a sensation that I had never experienced before, and one that I fervently hope I will never experience again.

I'd gotten into the habit of carrying a bottle of aspirin pills with me (several years before we had done a show with a cardiologist, and he had said it was a good idea to always carry some aspirin, just in case) and I quickly popped two of them. Later they told me that it was a good thing that I took the aspirin. I can't swear that the aspirin saved my life, but it made me feel slightly less helpless.

Despite the aspirin, the Sumo wrestler wouldn't quit pushing the box into my chest. I forced myself to accept the fact that I was in trouble. I pulled over into the parking lot of a former hospital, called 911 on my cell phone and was promptly connected to a dispatcher on the other side of the river. When I told her that I was in Cold Spring, and that I was having a heart attack, she told me that she would reroute my call to a dispatcher in Putnam County. That was nice of her, because if she'd sent an ambulance from where she was in Orange County, which is on the west side of the river, I'd still be waiting.

Two seconds later, I heard the sirens. First a local police officer arrived, followed almost immediately by an ambulance. It turned out the ambulance was practically around the corner from where I had parked. Two women, an emergency medical technician (EMT) and a paramedic, jumped out of the ambulance. They gave me a quick exam, put an oxygen mask over my face and helped me get into the ambulance. On the way to the hospital, they gave me nitroglycerin pills, which reduced the pain somewhat. My imaginary Sumo wrestler was still pushing down on the box, crushing my chest, and it hurt.

Nevertheless, the ambulance team was extremely professional, and I felt that I was in good hands. I began to relax and thought that maybe I'd dodged the bullet. Maybe it was just indigestion or constipation. Yeah, I thought, this is all a lot of fuss over nothing.

No such luck. When we arrived at the Hudson Valley Hospital Center, the ER physician told me they were going to run some tests. They hooked me up to an electrocardiogram (EKG), and I felt like I was in an episode of "Grey's Anatomy."

As it happened, Dr. Alan Slater – one of the area's top cardiologists – was just leaving the hospital after visiting with his patients. By habit, Dr. Slater always exits through the ER, and when the attending physician told him I was having chest pains, he made a beeline for me. I've gotten to know Dr. Slater very well since that night, but at that moment, he seemed a tad too serious for my taste. He reminded me of Mr. Spock explaining why the ship is about to explode ...

I'll always remember his first words to me: "Mr. Bennett, I don't like the look of your EKG. I'm going to watch it for a few more minutes. If things don't improve ..."

I thought, "Okay, he's a straight shooter, doesn't mince words. Maybe he'll decide that my EKG isn't so bad and he'll send me home. On the other hand, what did he mean by, 'If things don't improve?' That doesn't sound good."

He kept looking at my EKG, but I could tell by the look on his face that things hadn't improved. He told me he was going to inject me with a clot-busting drug. If that didn't do the trick, he was going to have the ambulance take me to the Westchester Medical Center, where they could run a catheter into me and manually bust up the clot, pretty much the same way that a plumber opens a clogged drain.

He gave me the injection, and we waited 30 minutes. Miraculously, the pain went away. I was out of the woods, I thought. Dr. Slater tells me that they're going to keep me at the hospital for a couple of days and see how everything goes.

To make a long story short, I developed an infection in my arm and my temperature shot up to 103.6 degrees, which is hot enough to melt cheese, and certainly hot enough to scramble my brain. Eventually, when they got the infection under control, they sent me home. A couple of weeks later, Dr. Slater scheduled me for a nuclear stress test, which sounds like something they should have done at Fukushima before they turned on the reactor.

The stress test was pretty cool. They shot me up with a special dye that lets them see how well (or poorly) the blood is flowing through my arteries. You get to watch it on a video screen while they're doing it. It's very cool. Sure enough, there was a crimp in one of my arteries. The crimp was making it hard for the blood to get to my heart. The doctors inserted a stent, which is a tiny device that basically props open the artery, and I've been fine ever since. My artery looks like the Holland Tunnel, except it's not filled with trucks on their way to New Jersey.

Here's an odd detail: Dr. Slater's partner, Dr. Richard Becker, had been a regular on our radio show several years before, and it was Dr. Becker who had recommended carrying aspirin around, just in case. In a weird way, those guys had been working to save my life before I even knew it!

ONLY *ONE* STENT?

Since having my heart attack, I've discovered there is a pecking order among heart attack survivors. One of my wife's aunts came up to me and asked me how I was feeling. Then she says, "You only got *one* stent? I've got *four*. My friend Louie has *six*. Are you sure you had a heart attack?"

And there are the people who had open-heart surgery. They show you their scars and brag about how many stitches they got. One of my relatives opened his shirt proudly and said, "Four hundred stitches. And that's just outside. There's another four hundred inside. That's real surgery!"

Wow, eight hundred stitches? I have jackets with fewer stitches than that. But the truth is that I'm happy – no, make that delighted – to have "gotten off easy."

A) As much as I admire the folks working in hospitals, I prefer sleeping at home, and B) I'm incredibly grateful just to be alive. Twenty years ago, it might have been a different story. You'd be reading my obituary instead of this book. My obituary would have been shorter, but probably not as funny. Then again, who knows? Somewhere out there, somebody is writing hysterically funny obits.

GRACE FROM YORKTOWN

The next best thing about my heart attack, apart from not dying, was that I was back on the air ten days later. While I was away, Kacey had told listeners that I was "under the weather," which I guess is better than saying I was under sedation.

As I prepared to return, I thought about what I would say to explain my absence. In radio, ten days is a long time for a talk-show host to be away from his microphone. I worried that if people knew that I had been seriously ill, they would see me as flawed or diminished. I realize now that it sounds crazy, but those were my thoughts at the time. I had become fearful, which is not a good thing for a radio host.

I was leaning towards not saying anything, until my son Michael, who is a DJ on our sister station, K-104.7 FM, asked me pointedly what I planned to tell my listeners.

When I told him that I probably wouldn't say anything, he urged me to reconsider. He was 23 at the time, but he has great instincts. He made a strong argument in favor of honesty – which, in all honesty, is almost always the best policy – and told me that speaking candidly about my experience would be a genuine service for the station's listeners.

It didn't take him long to convince me. I told the audience the story about my heart attack, talked about the excellent treatment I had received (only one stent!), and reassured everyone that I was feeling great.

Not long afterward, I received an email from a longtime listener. I call her "Grace from Yorktown," mostly because her name is Grace and she's from Yorktown. She told me that she had recently been diagnosed with heart disease, but that she had been afraid to undergo a procedure that would help her. After listening to me talk about my heart attack on the radio, she figured that if I could get through it and wind up okay, she could, too.

I've had several listeners tell me similar stories in the years since my heart attack, but Grace's story has always stayed with me. Not long afterward, the station sponsored a boat ride up the Hudson for listeners. A woman and her husband walk up to me.

She's wearing a blouse and I can see the top of what seems to be a long scar running down her chest. "Hi, I'm Grace from Yorktown," she says. Then her husband shakes my hand and says, "Thanks for saving my wife's life."

Her heart disease had been more advanced than mine, and required major surgery to fix. Needless to say, I was thrilled. I've invited Grace and her husband to several charity events that I host for local organizations like Go Red for Women and the Red Tie Club. I tell the story of how I met Grace, and introduce her to the audience. I call her my "closer," because after she talks, there's not much more for me to say.

I honestly don't know if talking about my heart attack on the radio actually saved lives, but if it helped a couple of people get the medical attention they needed, then I'm satisfied. Michael, thanks for making sure I did the right thing!

Part Nine

MAKING WAVES

MISSING PARTS?

If you've been paying close attention – and I know you have been – then you've probably noticed that this book skips from "Part Two" to "Part Nine," and you're probably wondering what happened to the missing parts.

If this were an episode of "The Sopranos," I'd suggest that you look for them in a landfill, under a light covering of topsoil. But that would be a lie. Here's the truth:

The missing parts of the book cover the years I spent wandering across some of the world's most dangerous and spectacular regions in my search for the meaning of life. I climbed the Himalayas, the Andes, the Alps and the Catskills. I took a pass on the Ramapo Mountains because I'd had a bad experience at a diner in Sloatsburg a long time ago.

All over the world I roamed, seeking existential meaning. It was a schlep, believe me. But I think it paid off. At the end of my spiritual journey, I learned that you can search the planet from top to bottom and still not find what you're looking for if you keep your eyes closed.

Did I forget to mention that I was wearing a blindfold during the entire trek? That was part of the deal I made with the travel agent, whose name I won't mention.

I hope that you can see where this story is leading. When she removed the blindfold, helped me out of the shipping crate and told me that I was back home in the Hudson Valley, I cried. Not because I realized that I'd probably never traveled out of Putnam County, but because I had learned an important lesson: Never let anyone blindfold you and put you in a shipping crate, even if they tell you it's for your own good.

I also learned another important lesson: Not every story has to make sense, or even have a point. Sometimes a story is just a nice way to kill the time. A story is like a journey. How you get there matters more than where you go.

By now, hopefully, you've realized why the book skips from "Part Two" to "Part Nine." The answer is simple: Because I knew that I would have to explain it and I wanted an excuse to tell you a funny story, even if it made absolutely no sense whatsoever.

THE DAILY GRIND

I am told that people love hearing about the trivial details and arcane minutiae of life in the media industry. Notice that I'm now calling it the "media industry" instead of the "radio business." To my untutored ear, "media industry" seems so much more 21st century than "radio business," which evokes images of a guy wearing a mackinaw trying to hoist an antenna during a thunderstorm.

But here are the cold hard facts: No matter what they told you in high school, radio is not electromagnetic energy. It's entirely magical, and yes, I really am inside your radio, and there is no studio. Now that we've gotten that out of the way, let's get down to the nitty-gritty.

The alarm goes off at 4:45 a.m. I live in Beacon and the studio is in Fishkill. The studio used to be in Peekskill, but it moved to Fishkill in 1998. You getting all this? There's going to be a quiz tomorrow.

It used to take me about 20 minutes to commute to work, but then I bought a house that's closer to the studio. I'm so close, in fact, that I can practically walk to work, but I really don't like walking on dark country roads when I'm still half asleep. Plus I would miss the daily thrill of fumbling noisily for my car keys while everyone else in the house is sleeping.

The weekday show, "*Mike & Kacey* in the Morning," starts at 5:30 a.m. The Saturday show, which I do solo, begins at 6 a.m. Kacey and I use Electro-Voice RE20 broadcast microphones and Sony MDR7506 professional headphones, both of which are considered the industry standards.

We never take meal breaks (What, never? Well, hardly ever ...) and sip water sparingly, mostly to avoid mad dashes to the bathroom. Drinking soda on the air is not a good idea because frankly nobody wants to hear you burping.

To be honest, we do occasionally bring food and non-alcoholic beverages into the studio, but it's a rare event. Sometimes an advertiser will deliver samples and we will "eat" or "drink" the product on air. One time, an advertiser sent us live lobsters, which was interesting ...

Guzzling booze while working is absolutely verboten, both by company policy and by common sense. It's hard enough doing the job when you're sober; it's impossible when you're half in the bag. ToRWUI (talking on radio while under the influence) would be a CE (career-ender), FS (for sure).

And I did manage to lock myself out of the studio on a cold wintry day. Luckily for me, I was able to attract the attention of a station employee who was inside warming his hands over the copying machine and he let me back in, after checking my ID and asking me to say, "Newburgh, two-hour delay, no morning kindergarten," to verify that I actually was Mike Bennett.

POOL VOLLEYBALL

Lots of people ask me, "Mike, what do you do when you're not on the radio?" My simple answer is: I play pool volleyball.

What is pool volleyball? As the name suggests, it's volleyball that you play in a pool. I play year-round at All Sport Health & Fitness Club in Fishkill. When you play pool volleyball, you're in a separate category. It's like visiting another world. All of the players are very different. It's an eclectic group, for sure. We range in age from 18 to 85. We also range far and wide in our abilities, which is a nice way of saying that we're not particularly athletic. I doubt the Olympic Pool Volleyball Committee will be recruiting from our ranks anytime soon.

In the winter we play in the indoor pool and in the summer we play in the outdoor pool. And we don't use a volleyball, we use a beach ball. Or something that looks like a beach ball. I'm not sure what it really is.

We play most every afternoon. People show up, we divide ourselves into two teams and we play. It's a hoot. We make up our own rules, and we change them whenever we feel like it. We rarely have arguments, because the goal of pool volleyball is having fun. We decided a long time ago that you can smack the ball as many times as you want to before sending it over the net to the other team. Sometimes we look like a bunch of seals. We try to keep the ball moving. There really isn't any set strategy, and we rarely keep score. We're as disorganized as possible, which probably explains why we've been able to stick together over the years. We laugh a lot, and we generally drive the other members of the club crazy.

MIKE & KACEY IN THE MORNING

It always feels a little weird when someone asks me to explain the "history" of *Mike & Kacey in the Morning*, because to me the show it isn't "history" – it's a big chunk of my life. That being said, we've been doing the show for such a long time that it probably qualifies as "history" by now.

So let's begin at the beginning. The WHUD morning show began in 1972. The show's first host was Joe O'Brien, a veteran of WMCA and one of the original WMCA Good Guys. For those of you too young to remember, the Good Guys were pioneers of pop radio, introducing The Beatles and other great bands to millions of listeners. Joe did the morning show here at WHUD for 14 years, until 1986. His successor was Ed Baer, another former Good Guy. Ed also did the show for 14 years, until 2000.

Kacey Morabito and I have been hosting the show since 2000. Here's where the story gets a little complicated, so stay with me. Or lie down and take a nap, whichever you prefer.

I was the show's solo host for about a month – a very *lonely* month, I might add – before Kacey joined the lineup. Kacey and I had met originally in the early 1980s, when she was an intern at the station. According to Kacey, I unlocked the station door for her on her first day at work. I don't actually remember doing that, but I'm more than happy to take a tiny grain of credit for helping Kacey launch her career in radio.

Those of you who have met Kacey know that she is incredibly talented and energetic, so it was no surprise to us when our young intern left the station for greener pastures and higher paychecks. Such is life in the radio biz. *Que sera, sera.*

Kacey and I stayed in touch over the years – the radio community is like a large extended family, and you tend to keep bumping into the same people – and when the station found out that she was available, we jumped at the chance to hire her as co-host of the show.

By the time you read this book, we'll be celebrating our 14th year as co-hosts of the show. I'm fairly confident that we'll break the records held by our illustrious predecessors, but only time will tell.

Someone recently said we were like George Clooney and Sandra Bullock in the movie "Gravity," minus the 3D explosions. I take that as a compliment, although anyone who thinks I resemble George Clooney needs their vision checked. On the other hand, I can see some similarities between Kacey and Sandra Bullock. And I *do* mean that as a compliment!

NATURAL CHEMISTRY

One question I'm frequently asked is, "What's it like working with the same person, day in and day out, for so many years?" My response to that is simple: Kacey and I have a natural chemistry, and doing the show with her doesn't feel like work. Honestly, I can't remember ever being bored during all of my years of doing the show. I guess that's one of the secrets of longevity – if you love what you're doing, it's easy to keep doing it for a long time.

There's some luck involved, too. Prior to 2000, Kacey and I had never worked together on the same show. We were a little anxious and we wondered if our individual personalities would mesh well on the air. But we hit it off immediately. As I said, it's a matter of chemistry. If it's not there, you can't fake it. But when you've got it, it's like pure gold. Or high-grade plutonium.

We have a couple of techniques for keeping our on-air relationship fresh. First, we try never to speak – or even see other – until we're ready to start the show. We begin our banter three or four minutes before the show goes live. It helps us warm up our voices and it builds momentum. When the show officially begins at 5: 30 a.m., we're usually halfway into a conversation that began a few minutes earlier. Typically, we're laughing or sharing a story. We usually backtrack and explain to our listeners what made us laugh or we retell whatever story we were sharing. We try to engage our listeners and bring them into the conversation.

Second, we don't follow a script. We have a format and we have a schedule, but within those parameters, we're free to say virtually anything we want to say. I think the fact that we're continuously improvising – working without a net, so to speak – gives the show a natural quality. It sounds like spontaneous conversation because that's exactly what it is. We're making it up as we go, on the spot, live from the studio.

An example from a recent show: Kacey was talking. I looked up and saw a gigantic praying mantis on the outside window. I broke in and said, "Kacey, I'm sorry for interrupting you, but you would not believe the size of the praying mantis sitting on our window!" We spent the next couple of minutes talking about praying mantises. Then listeners began calling in with *their* praying mantis stories. Pretty soon, the theme of the show had become "Wacky Bugs I Have Known," and everyone was sharing stories of odd bugs and weird insects. It was hysterical, and totally spontaneous.

Some radio hosts work from scripts – you can buy jokes and scripted patter – but we've always preferred inventing our own material. We like to say that living in the area is all the prep we really need. And it's true. If you live in the Hudson Valley, you know that there's always something going on here that's offbeat and interesting.

We're proud to live and work in the Hudson Valley. Kacey was born here. I migrated from Brooklyn as a toddler. We're both solidly anchored in the region, professionally and personally. Perhaps "anchored" is the wrong word. Maybe we're more like barnacles. But seriously, I cannot imagine a better place to raise a family and host a radio show. And I cannot imagine a better co-host than Kacey!

METHOD TO OUR MADNESS

Despite our freestyle approach to the show, I would not describe our method as pure chaos. Even when you're improvising, you still need some kind of basic structure. Before the show begins, we fill in a format sheet. There are three circles on the sheet, labeled 6:00, 7:00 and 8:00. Each circle represents an hour of the show. Inside each circle, we write down a few words describing what we plan to do in that hour.

For example, in the first hour, in addition to reading the traffic and weather, we read horoscopes.

In the next hour, we read birthday announcements and play recordings of local school children reciting the Pledge of Allegiance, which is one of our most popular features. We go to schools around the region and record classrooms reciting the Pledge of Allegiance. Then we play a different recording every morning. People love it.

We also announce our giveaway contests. We have four or five contests every morning. The first, our "Early Bird Contest," is at 5:45 a.m. We throw out a question and invite listeners to call us with an answer. A typical question might be, "What was the top grossing film at the box office this weekend?" Sometimes we ask specific questions, and sometimes we ask open-ended questions.

The seventh caller (we picked the number seven because our station's radio frequency is 100.7 MHz) gets to answer the question. We take the call while a song is playing and we record the conversation. I edit the recording (usually to remove the caller's "ums" and "ahs") and then we play it on air as the next song is beginning. We have to work fast, but it helps us keep the audience engaged.

The prizes are usually tickets to an upcoming local event, so the contest also serves as a promotion for whatever group is staging the event. For example, we recently gave away tickets to the Great Jack-O-Lantern Blaze, an annual event at Van Cortlandt Manor sponsored by the Historic Hudson Valley Organization. It's a cool event, and draws big crowds every year. There are literally thousands of blazing jack-o-lanterns. It's quite a spectacle!

LOVING THE HUDSON VALLEY

I've talked a lot about the Hudson River Valley in this book, assuming rather blithely that most readers are familiar with the area. My editor suggested (rather optimistically, I think) that people from other parts of the nation (or even other parts of the world!) might read this book, and that some of those readers might be clueless about the region. At his urging, I have added a brief but poignant description of our beautiful area.

The Hudson River Valley National Heritage Area starts at the northern border of New York City and extends north to Albany, give or take a couple of miles. It covers ten counties: Westchester,

Rockland, Orange, Putnam, Ulster, Dutchess, Greene, Columbia, Albany and Rensselaer.

The region includes, according to the Hudson River Valley Institute, "2.5 million residents, five National Historic Sites, 58 National Historic Landmarks, 89 historic districts, and over 1,000 sites listed on the National Register of Historic Places." Wow!

According to the institute (and who wants to argue with an institute?), our region "is one of the America's most important scenic, cultural, economic, and historic regions. For many of the European colonists, the 315-mile long river was America's first river, discovered by Henry Hudson in 1609."

The Algonquins, who apparently had no use for Henry Hudson, called the southern part of the river "Mohicanituk," which meant "the River That Flows Both Ways." Some days, it certainly seems to flow in both directions, especially if you're in a boat and your motor dies while you're in the middle of the river.

Speaking as someone who has lived in the Hudson Valley for more than 60 years, I can say that it is certainly, in my humble estimation, one of the most beautiful places on earth.

On the river's east side, I'm partial to Beacon, the town I've lived in since 1985. I'm also fond of Peekskill and Yonkers – and pretty much everything in between. Despite the suburbanization of Westchester, you don't have to drive very far to feel as though you're in a primeval forest. In fact, you haven't really experienced the Hudson Valley until you've been lost for hours on one of our winding back roads.

On the west side of the river, I'm a big fan of Highland Mills. That's where I grew up. I love the fact that my nephew now owns my childhood home on Birchwood Drive. I also like Monroe, where many of my early friends lived. In fact, some of them still live there!

I also love Warwick, which is practically on the border of New York and New Jersey. It's a very pretty town, almost too good to be true: green pastures, rolling hills, sparkling blue lakes, old farmhouses and country stores.

One of my favorite local landmarks is the U.S. Military Academy at West Point. The original fortress at West Point was strategically located at a sharp bend in the river. During the Revolutionary War, the rebels stretched a chain across the Hudson to stop the British fleet from using the river. When you visit West Point, you can see some the chain's enormous links, which are now part of a monument overlooking the river.

West Point is a great destination, with all kinds of events and activities, from sports to music to theater. Whenever I visit West Point, the castle-like buildings make me feel as though I've traveled back in time to the 12th century. All that's missing is jousting knights. Actually, you can see jousting at the annual Renaissance Faire in Sterling Forest, which is about 15 miles south of West Point.

Every so often, someone will ask me if I ever considered relocating to a larger market where I could make more money. Sure, I've considered it, but then I take one look around me and remember that I'm already living in one of the nicest places on earth. I feel grateful, blessed and fortunate. I also feel thirsty after all of this writing, so please excuse me while I get a diet soda ...

GRAMMAR AND OTHER NUISANCES

Every morning, my alarm goes off at 4:45 a.m. I forget if I already mentioned that. At this point, I'm just typing and hoping my editor will turn it into English before the book is actually printed. I'm also hoping that my editor has the patience of Job and Mother Teresa combined. A passing knowledge of grammar would be helpful, too. Grammar is not my strength. And calling it my weakness would be unfair to weaklings.

I never understood formal grammar, in any language. Maybe that was part of my problem. I could never pass any of the foreign languages that I took in school, so they kept switching me to a different language, hoping that I'd be better at the new language than the previous language. For me, all foreign languages were equally impossible. I think that I took every language offered in the New York State school system, with the possible exception of Urdu.

To be perfectly candid, I have no idea if they teach Urdu in New York State, but I just wanted to type the word and see it in print. Okay, moving right along ... where were we? Yes, language and grammar. Both are great mysteries to me, which is odd when you consider that I earn my bread by talking. Fortunately, the ability to speak is hard-wired into our brains. I don't know if that's true or not, but it seems very scientific.

One thing I learned while writing this book is never try to edit your own writing. Hire an editor to do that. Or hire a chimpanzee, whichever is handy.

But seriously, if your goal is writing, then just write. Don't worry while you're writing about whether what you're writing is good, bad or indifferent. Let history be your judge.

After Shakespeare died, the next generation of English writers took turns making fun of his plays and telling their pals that Shakespeare was a bum and an embarrassment to the civilized world. It took the next generation after that to "discover" that Shakespeare was pretty good after all. Maybe the writers who spent their careers trying to outdo

Shakespeare should have spent more time writing and less time bad-mouthing him. There's a lesson there somewhere, I'm sure ...

At any rate, my point is that most of life is like writing or talking on the radio. You do your best, you try to be generally pleasant to most people and you let history decide if you were any good or not.

And sometimes history gets it wrong. *Moby-Dick,* one of the greatest novels ever written – certainly the greatest American novel ever written – was out of print for years. I mean, let's face it, *Moby-Dick* is a long book. Way too long. Makes a great door stop.

But the characters in *Moby-Dick* remind me of people I've met. Ishmael is the guy sitting next to you on the bus who just won't shut up even when you're trying to take a nap. Queequeg is the strong quiet guy in high school who protects you from bullies. Starbuck is the kid who everyone thinks is cool but then turns out to be a hopeless wuss. Ahab is the crazy shop teacher you have in seventh grade who screams at you for not sweeping sawdust off the circular saw and spends most of the day reading weird magazines about aliens and sea monsters.

The really amazing thing about *Moby-Dick* is that there was no sequel. Sure, <<SPOILER ALERT>>, everybody except Ishmael dies at the end, but that never stopped anyone from writing a sequel to a bestselling book.

If *Moby-Dick* were written today, there definitely would be a sequel and a full line of products. Ishmael would be a late-night talk show host. Queequeg also would have his own show, probably on the Discovery Channel. Starbuck would be selling mocha latte and Ahab would be managing the New York Rangers.

EVERYTHING YOU NEED TO KNOW ABOUT *HAMLET* IN 90 SECONDS

And while we're on the topic of great literature, here's another thing that ticks me off: Why people have a problem understanding why Hamlet is A) sad and B) indecisive.

Okay, part of the problem is the way they taught us *Hamlet* in school. The teacher handed out copies of the play to us on Friday afternoon and told us to read it over the weekend because there would be a quiz on Monday. Naturally, nobody except Debbie Do Right and Andy Apple Polisher bothered to open the book, even though it had a picture of a handsome young guy wearing tights and talking to a skull on the cover.

It took me years to get through the play, and that was only after someone told me what was going on. So I'm going to make life easier for you (or your kids) and give you my two cents on why Prince Hamlet is sad and indecisive. Don't worry, my explanation will be brief and to the point.

A) Hamlet is sad because right before the play begins, he's away at college and he finds out that his dad, who's never been sick a day in his life, has mysteriously died. I think we can all agree that getting bad news like that when you're away from home would probably make you sad. I know that it would make me sad. It kills me when people say, "Oh, he just should have gotten over it." That is ridiculous. My dad died when I was a little boy, and I still haven't gotten over it.

The other reason why Hamlet is sad is because he's the prince, and technically, he should have become the next king and inherited all the cool stuff that goes along with being the king. But no, his father's creepy brother Claudius has married Hamlet's mom, and now Mr. Creepy is king and Hamlet has bupkis.

Let's review, Hamlet's dad has died mysteriously and he's been screwed out of a fortune. I think that any reasonable person might be upset under those circumstances.

B) Hamlet is indecisive because a ghost who looks like his dead father tells him to murder the king of Denmark. If a ghost suddenly shows up and tells you to kill the most powerful guy in the country, would you just go and do it ... or would you maybe think it over a couple a times and figure out a bunch of excuses for not murdering the king? Me, I'd be thinking long and hard about what I ate right before I saw the ghost ... maybe it was all a hallucination caused by a really intense case of indigestion or those weird looking mushrooms on the pizza.

And then there's a practical matter. If Hamlet runs downstairs and kills the king right after listening to the ghost, the play would be 10 minutes long. Imagine how the original audiences – gangs of drunken rowdy Elizabethans – would have reacted.

They would have rioted. They would have ripped up the seats and thrown them, along with rotten vegetables and empty bottles of cheap wine, at the actors. And worse, they might have asked for their money back.

On some level, I think that Shakespeare knew that he had to write a longer play and pack it with plenty of action – there's a stabbing, a drowning, a pirate attack and a pretty wild swordfight in the last scene – to keep audiences from revolting.

As I said, it took me years to figure out *Hamlet*, mostly because nobody told me that it's basically a very simple story that makes perfect sense if you think about it for two seconds. It also helps to see the play performed on stage, or to watch one of the 8,000 movie versions of it.

And don't worry about the quiz. I failed the quiz, and here I am, years later, writing about Shakespeare. Oh, the irony … Good night, sweet prince!

DISEMBODIED VOICES AND SHADOWS ON THE SCREEN

As you can tell by now, I live a large part of my life on the radio. Or maybe it's more accurate to say, "in the radio," since if you're a listener, it must seem as though I'm in your radio. Don't worry, I'm not. Maybe I could squeeze myself into one of the old mahogany radio cabinets from the 1930s, the kind our grandparents had in the living room. Those were the days when the radio was a piece of furniture.

I'd have to lose a lot of weight to squeeze into a modern radio receiver. And forget about MP3 players. I did a TV show briefly, but I never felt as though I was living on the television. Radio is my home, plain and simple. You can put that on my tombstone, but please wait until I'm actually dead.

I do love watching TV, however. If it's a show about sports or music, I'll watch it. My all-time favorite show is "24." I also like "The Big Bang Theory," "Suits," "Cops," "Blue Bloods" and "Judge Judy," which is the only show that I DVR five days a week. My favorite mini-series was "Lonesome Dove," with Robert Duval. I think Duval is one of the greatest actors of all time. And it's always nice seeing him in a cowboy hat.

FUZZY RECEPTION

When I was kid, there were far fewer shows on TV. Heck, there were far fewer channels. At our home in Highland Mills, we got three channels: 2, 4, 5. Sometimes we got Channel 7. Once in a while we'd pick up Channel 11, and very rarely, Channel 13. That was it. And the rest was static.

So basically, we didn't watch much TV when we were growing up. We went to the movies as much as possible, and we loved them.

The movies were also an education. I learned more about the Revolutionary War, the Civil War and World War II by watching movies than I ever learned in school. I don't remember reading anything about the Crimean War in school, but I remember seeing "The Charge of the Light Brigade" with Errol Flynn and Olivia de Havilland. Come to think of it, I must have seen the movie on TV, since it was made in 1936. But it still taught me an important lesson: When it's guys with cannons versus guys carrying lances on horseback, don't bet on the guys with lances to win, even if Errol Flynn is one of the guys carrying a lance.

It was always hard for me to believe that Errol Flynn would ever get killed at the end of a movie. He also gets killed at the end of "They Died With Their Boots On." That's the movie where he plays General George Custer, who led his cavalry troopers into a bloody massacre at the Battle of Little Big Horn.

I'm sure that somebody at Warner Brothers argued in favor of keeping him alive so he could ride off into the sunset with Olivia de Havilland. And I like to think that some kind soul said, "No, we must stick to the historical facts or thirty years from now Mike Bennett will flunk American History in high school." I passed the course by the skin of my teeth, in large part thanks to watching old movies on television.

THE BRITISH INVASION

I also learned a lot from the James Bond movies that we saw in theaters. I have nothing against Roger Moore or Daniel Craig, but for me and for millions of other Baby Boomers, Sean Connery will always be the quintessential James Bond. Everything that I know about women, exploding briefcases and mar- tinis (shaken, not stirred) can be traced to my three favorite Bond movies: "Dr. No," "From Russia With Love" and "Goldfinger." Not coincidentally, they were the first three, and in my opinion, the best of the bunch.

As much as we loved James Bond, we loved The Beatles even more. And unlike Bond, they were real people.

It always amazes me that when I hear a Beatles song today, I can usually remember exactly what I was doing when I first heard the song on WABC back in the 1960s. When the early albums were released, I was in junior high school. The rest of them were released while I was in high school. In fact, I gradu- ated from high school the same year that the Beatles broke up. No wonder I didn't want to go to college. If we couldn't look forward to new Beatles albums, what was the point of going to school?

MISSING THE FEAR OF FAILURE

Every day, I thank God that I have a job that I enjoy doing. My career in radio has been a blessing, and I mean that sincerely. I roll out of bed in the morning, find a clean shirt to wear and pretty soon I'm yammering over the airwaves. Did I mention that my alarm goes off at 4:45? Apart from the early hours, it's the best job in the world.

I recently read *Outliers* by Malcolm Gladwell, in which he says that on average, it takes about 10,000 hours of practice to get really good at doing something. Well, I've definitely passed the 10,000-hour mark doing radio. I'm not going to say that spending all those hours sitting in a chair talking into a microphone has made me a great radio personality, but I can say that I've become very comfortable in my role.

Maybe comfortable isn't the right word. If you saw my chair, you'd know why. I think what I really mean is that I've become extremely confident that when I sit down and start talking, I'm not going to embarrass myself or the station.

My years of experience have definitely helped me to become smoother and calmer. I'm less easily perturbed or flustered. That's the upside. The downside is that it's hard to surprise me. I can't truthfully say that "I have seen it all," but I can say that I have seen quite a bit.

When I was younger and less experienced, I worried more. Like every performer, I harbored an abject fear of failure beneath my placid veneer. I spent years working to overcome my fears. I like to think that I managed to succeed in spite of them.

But here's the odd thing: When I think about it honestly, I know that on some weird level, I miss my old fears and anxieties. In some mysterious way, they were a stimulant – they kept me on edge. And when I triumphed over them, it was a real cause for celebration. I remember those early victories and I cherish them.

The downside of my present state of confidence is that I tend not to remember my performances. I don't think about what I'm doing. I just do it. It's like one of the Blue Angels once told me about flying aerobatic combat maneuvers upside down in an air show: "If you have to think about what you're doing, you're in trouble!"

That kind of instinctive approach to my work doesn't usually leave memories. At least it doesn't leave the kind of memories that were seared into my brain by disasters like mispronouncing the governor's name or accidentally locking myself out of the studio during a commercial break.

It's not like I'm running on autopilot. It's just that my perceptions of the job have changed over the years. At the beginning of my career, I felt as though I had to obsess over every individual frame of the movie that was my life. Now I'm simply sitting back and enjoying the movie. And eating popcorn, of course.

In a sense, writing this book has brought back some of my old fears and anxieties. Unlike doing a morning radio show, writing a book is not a walk in the park for me. It's more like a sprint up Mount Everest. I'm hoping that you will like this book, but I'm not absolutely certain that you won't hate it. In fact, part of me worries that I'll be awakened in the middle of the night by a blazing bonfire of books in my front yard.

Come to think of it, though, you'd need a lot of copies of my book to make a decent bonfire. That means that if you want to burn a bonfire's worth of books in my front yard, you'll need to buy at least 200 copies. If that's your plan, call me and we can discuss a bulk discount.

IMPORTANT DATES
IN HISTORY

TIMELINE

Everything that I know about history I learned from watching old Warner Bros. movies on the days when I could talk my mom into letting me stay home from school. I'm sure they gave us textbooks at some point in high school, but I don't recall ever actually opening one up and reading it. For all I knew, the pages could have been blank. Or written in Greek. It didn't make any difference to me. At the end of the year, I returned my textbooks to my teachers in the exact same condition they'd been in when I got them – unopened and unread.

Thank goodness for Jack Warner and Errol Flynn, or I wouldn't know anything about the Spanish Armada, the Charge of the Light Brigade or the Battle of Little Big Horn.

Since it would be a shame – a crying shame – if you were to find yourself abroad in the big wide world without a minimal knowledge of history, I have provided the following list of important dates. A list of important figs will be included at the end of my next book, and a list of important prunes will be featured in the next book after that, assuming that

I haven't been remanded to a psychiatric hospital for evaluation.

IT ALL STARTED with the Big Bang. Nobody is certain of when this actually happened, although the consensus in the scientific community is that "It was probably a Tuesday afternoon – on one of those spring days that feels kind of like autumn." The important thing to remember about the Big Bang is that *everything else happened afterward* – although Mrs. Seymour Blatt of Nutley, NJ could swear she remembers eating a really good corned beef sandwich at the Red Apple Rest a full three weeks earlier.

4.5 billion B.C. – Earth is formed. It's an "oblate spheroid," meaning it's a bit wider than it is tall. My kind of planet!

3 billion B.C. – The most primitive forms of life arise. Among them: bacteria, blue-green algae and people who illegally park in handicapped spots.

4.4 million B.C. – The earliest hominids appear. A palpable sense of dread pervades the universe.

(Somewhere in here, by the way, Slim Jims come along. This, in itself, is not such an important fact. However, very soon after the discovery of Slim Jims, people notice that they are extremely thirsty. This leads to the invention of water, which is considered kind of a big deal, because as we now know, without water, there'd be no Yoo-Hoo.)

70,000 B.C. – First use of fire. Until this point, nobody had any idea what that Pointer Sisters song even meant.

(Long period of boredom, unless you think farming is interesting.)

2,000 B.C. – Hyskos invaders drive Egyptians from Lower Egypt, most likely in a pea green Pinto they borrowed from their friend, Jerry.

600 B.C. – Fed up with people continually mispronouncing his name, Babylonian king Nebuchadnezzar loses it and destroys Jerusalem.

(Another long period of boredom, unless you think the rise and fall of great civilizations is interesting.)

50 B.C. – Caesar crosses Rubicon to fight Pompey, but not before pausing to do that annoying water sprinkler dance.

THE YEAR ONE – Jesus Christ is born, changing the world in countless ways and finally giving people something to say when they hit their thumb with a hammer.

1066 – Battle of Hastings. William the Conqueror introduces French wine to the Britons, who, having subsisted all this time on Boone's Farm Apple Wine, are understandably grateful.

1150 – Universities of Paris and Oxford founded in France and England. First order of business at both schools: set tuition so high that $400 textbooks seem like a bargain in comparison.

1215 – King John signs the Magna Carta at Runnymede, laying the foundation for modern constitutional democracies. They had to use Runnymede because they'd already drunk the thick, syrupy stuff and all they had left was the thin, runny leftovers. All I remember about King John was that Claude Rains played him in the movie, "Robin Hood," and that he spent a good deal of the movie gnawing on a huge haunch of barbecued venison while leering lewdly at Olivia de Haviland, who played Maid Marion. I remember that he also instructed Basil Rathbone to find Robin Hood and kill him, which seemed unlikely since Errol Flynn played Robin and he had gotten top billing in the movie. "Find Robin Hood or you'll spend the rest of your career in B-pictures!" John screams. Basil Rathbone didn't capture Robin Hood, but he did become famous playing Sherlock Holmes, so I guess it all worked out.

1325 – The Renaissance begins in Italy. Soon after, 25 million people die in the Black Plague, causing at least one person to comment: "How ironic is it that so many people are dying during the Renaissance, which, after all, means rebirth?" (Nobody laughed then, either.)

Other Renaissance highlights:

- DaVinci paints the Mona Lisa. It goes on to become the best-known painting in the world, mostly because it's so much fun to draw a mustache on.

- Michelangelo sculpts his famous David, who, if he could talk, would probably have a *lot* to say about shrinkage.

- The philosophy known as humanism catches on bigtime. Humanists were all about returning to the classics for guidance. I can totally relate. I watched a ton of old *Three Stooges* episodes in preparation for writing this book.

1387 – Chaucer writes *The Canterbury Tales,* which was once considered a big deal but is now used primarily to make really awful spellers feel better about themselves. "Two yonge knyghtes liggynge by and by." Really? I spelled better than that in preschool, dude.

1543 – Nicolaus Copernicus publishes *De revolutionibus orbium coelestium,* in which he posits that the sun, not the earth, is the center of the universe. This theory remains in vogue until 2010, when Kim Kardashian becomes the official center of the universe.

1582 – Pope Gregory XIII implements the Gregorian calendar. From this point on, a year is 10 minutes and 48 seconds shorter. Feel free to use this as an excuse next time you're 10 minutes late for an appointment.

1630 – Massachusetts Bay Colony is established. Minutes later, the colonial legislature passes a law prohibiting the use of the "r" sound.

1704 – The Boston News Letter – the first newspaper in America – is published, and the first fight over who gets to do the Crypto-Quip takes place.

1729 – Isaac Newton's Principia is translated from Latin to English, causing English-speaking readers to say, "Aha!", followed by: "I still don't get it."

1762 – Mozart tours Europe as a six-year-old prodigy. His contract rider stipulates that promoters provide herring in sour cream, Schlitz Malt Liquor beer and "absolutely no brown M&Ms."

1775 – The American Revolution begins, paving the way for unimaginable freedom, courageous exploration and Honey Boo Boo.

1776 – Washington crosses the Delaware on Christmas night. Turns out he had totally forgotten to get a present for Martha, and was hoping there'd be a Rite Aid open somewhere on the other side of the river.

1781 – Herschel discovers Uranus. I'm not gonna touch that one.

1794 – Eli Whitney invents the cotton gin, a mechanical contraption that reinvigorates the American cotton industry and extends the slavery system for another 70 years. And this is considered a good thing? I'm sure that Whitney was a bright guy, but we would've been better off if he'd spent his time improving the popcorn maker.

1800 – Alessandro Volta produces electricity for the first time, but its use is extremely limited until he can locate one of those little adapter thingies.

1803 – The U.S. doubles its size with the Louisiana Purchase. Two centuries later, Americans continue to double their size with Big Mac purchases.

1823 – The Monroe Doctrine warns European countries not to interfere in the Western Hemisphere. Tony Soprano sends Silvio Dante and Paulie Walnuts across the Atlantic, just to make sure Europe doesn't try anything funny.

1825 – The Erie Canal officially opens, linking New York City to the Great Lakes. There goes the neighborhood.

1826 – Joseph-Nicefore Niepce takes world's first photograph. His subjects – a few buildings and a pear tree – all say the same thing afterward: "Wait! Take another one! I blinked!"

1861 – U.S. Civil War begins. I have a question: If everybody's shooting at everybody else, how does that qualify as "civil"? It's time for truly civil wars, where combatants are so polite to their opponents that everybody gets bored and goes home.

1901 – First trans-Atlantic radio signal is sent. The full text of the historic exchange is presented here for posterity:

- wutup d00d?
- nada beeyotch!!!
- aight. l8r.

1903 – The Wright Brothers make their first successful flight at Kitty Hawk. An ugly altercation breaks out when Wilbur refuses to let Orville board with more than one carry-on bag.

1908 – Ford introduces the Model T, saying, "Someday, Fred MacMurray will invent Flubber and you'll really see this thing fly!"

1912 – The parachute is invented. Prior to this, it was significantly less enjoyable to jump out of an airplane.

1922 – Tomb of King Tut is found, causing wise-acres all over the world to say, "I didn't even know it was missing!"

1928 – With the invention of sliced bread, Western civilization reaches its apex.

1930 – Pluto is discovered, paving the way for the discovery of Goofy.

1932 – Scientists split the atom. Years later, they will claim never to have said, "What possible harm could come from this?"

1942 – The first t-shirt is unveiled, although several decades will elapse before the garment's potential is fully realized with the introduction of the now-classic "I'M WITH STUPID" design.

1945 – The Slinky is introduced, causing a national sensation and finally answering the age-old question: "What walks downstairs, alone or in pairs and makes a slinkity sound?"

1946 – The bikini bathing suit is introduced. Did I say the invention of sliced bread was the apex of Western civilization? I stand corrected.

1947 – Chuck Yeager breaks sound barrier, apologizes, promises to fix it, still hasn't.

1950 – First organ transplant performed. A malfunctioning Wurlitzer belonging to a Mrs. Clyde Fleen of Akron, Ohio is replaced by a brand new Hammond with a Leslie speaker.

1952 – Automobile seat belts are introduced. Inexplicably, more than half a century later, flight attendants still think we need to be shown how to use them.

1953 – Playboy magazine makes its debut, and it's a good thing, because man oh man, does that magazine have some great articles!

1956 – The TV remote control is invented, rendering the debilitating eight-foot march to the television little more than a chilling memory of a dark and horrific time.

1959 – "Kitchen debate" between Nixon and Krushchev. Main area of disagreement: Whether or not pasta should be broken in half before placing in boiling water.

1963 – First "Dr. Who" episode airs. The show is about a humanoid alien who explores the universe in a sentient, time-traveling spaceship that looks like an English police box. In other words, it is way more realistic than most reality shows.

1963 – A special telephone "hotline" is established between the U.S. and the U.S.S.R. In the first use of the historic hotline, Kennedy disguises his voice and calls Krushchev to ask if he has Prince Albert in a can.

1964 – The Beatles become popular in America. For our young readers, the Beatles were the band Paul McCartney played in before Wings. For our even younger readers, Wings was a band that sold a lot of records in the 70s. For our very young readers, records were how we used to listen to music before CDs were invented. For our very, very young readers, CDs were shiny discs, filled with music, which people bought back when people paid for music instead of illegally downloading it.

1969 – The Woodstock Music & Arts Fair draws 400,000 people to a farm in Sullivan County, NY. If you remember being there, you probably weren't.

1989 – President George H.W. Bush uses his position as the most powerful being on the planet to announce to the world that he does not like broccoli.

1991 – A 4,000-year-old man is found in the Alps. Betty White is rushed in to identify him.

1997 – Scientists clone a sheep, and the world breathes a sigh of relief as the horrifying possibility of a sheep shortage is eliminated once and for all.

2001 – Multimillionaire Dennis Tito becomes the world's first space tourist. He spends eight days on the International Space Station before being kicked off the craft for saying, "Open the pod bay doors, Hal" one too many times.

2002 – The dwarf planet Quaoar is discovered, roughly four billion miles from the sun. Later in the same year, the new planet's first Starbucks opens.

2004 – Facebook is launched, making it possible for people to appear busy while doing absolutely nothing of any value whatsoever.

2005 – YouTube is introduced. This is considered a powerful "game changer" in that people can now watch total strangers "twerking" on the other side of the planet.

2007 – Arctic sea ice hits record low, causing widespread concern about rising sea levels. Kentuckians, however, are heartened by the certainty that they will soon be the owners of valuable oceanfront property.

2011 – Population of the planet reaches seven billion, which explains why it's so hard to find a parking space nowadays.

2012 – The Mayan calendar reaches the end of its current cycle. There is absolutely no evidence that the Mayans – who relied on the calendar in countless ways – were worried about this event. So, it's completely understandable that our civilization, which is barely connected to Mayan culture, is consumed by fears about the end of the world.

2014 – A low point in Western civilization is reached with the publication of "Don't Pay the Ransom, I've Escaped: Memories of a Life on the Radio." And they said I'd never amount to anything!

AND NOW SOME *REALLY* IMPORTANT DATES

I hope you got a chuckle or two from my hysterical – I mean historical – timeline. But at the request of my friends and family, here are the really important dates in my life:

Oct 23rd, 1976 – I celebrate the nation's bicentennial year by marrying Mary Ellen (Liberty) Bell of Newburgh.

July 7th, 1982 – Our first child, Courtney Elizabeth, is born. Life will never be the same but it's all good!

March 20th, 1987 – Our second child, Michael Matthew arrives ... destined for great things, like his siblings.

August 8, 1989 – Matthew Edwin completes the Trifecta.

April 8, 2013 – Our first grandchild, Vivienne Ellen arrives. Life will never be the same, but it's all good. Where have I heard that before?

134

ACKNOWLEDGEMENTS

MERCI, GRACIAS AND GESUNDHEIT ...

Most of the material for this book was generated over a series of lunches at Rosy Tomorrow's, a great place in Danbury, Connecticut. I recommend it highly, especially if you're hungry and writing a book. Special thanks to Rebecca, who always smiled and brought us lots of ice water.

Large chunks of material were lifted from speeches that I gave to unwitting students at Mount Saint Mary College and Orange County Community College. May the good Lord forgive me for leading them astray.

Special thanks to Mike Barlow, who served as my writing coach. Mike and I were classmates at Monroe-Woodbury High School, and this project is a reunion, of sorts. Contrary to anything you might have heard, Mike definitely did not "ghostwrite" this book for me, because that would somehow suggest that I paid him, which I certainly did not.

Mike was ably assisted by his incredibly talented brother Bob, who also took no money for working on this project. In the distant past, both Mike and Bob were considered reasonably intelligent guys. Clearly, their decision to collaborate with me on this project knocks that idea into a cocked hat.

Not that anybody wears a cocked hat anymore. Unless you're a pirate, of course. I don't personally know any pirates, but if the book tour takes me to Somalia, I'll find out what they're wearing. Maybe the expression should be changed to "knocks that idea into a red fez." I'll ask around when I'm in Mogadishu and get back to you.

At least I got to use the word "fez" in the book. A small victory for all of you "Casablanca" fans out there. The original line was, "Here's looking at you, kid. Now take off the fez and sit down with me on the sofa." If you believe that, you'll probably enjoy my next book. Stay tuned!